T0246905

NO MORE FACEPLANTS

and *PLEASE—*
Hold the Oat Milk!

Finding the Funny When Life Gets Too Serious

MARY ANN HOYT

ISBN: 979-8-35095-814-0 paperback
ISBN: 979-8-35095-815-7 ebook

Also by Mary Ann Hoyt

In Heaven There's No Money, No Stuff—and No Porta-Potties
Coping With Life's Aggravations by Finding the Funny

Hashtags and Zoom Bewilder This Boomer
Finding the Funny While Aging

To those dear friends who said to me,
"You've got to write that down."

CONTENTS

INTRODUCTION

I figured I had no material left for a book #3. I retired from my nursing career years ago. It was now time to retire from writing, lay down my pen, and read other authors' books, sitting on a sandy beach with a glass of vino. Except—things kept happening in my life: silly things, stressful, absurd, and mundane. Memories of childhood, which fit into those same categories, resurrected themselves.

I realized that my head would explode if I didn't provide an exit ramp from my brain to paper. When I write, my rewards are many. The last line of the Nightingale Pledge, which we recited at our nursing school graduation was, "...devote myself to the welfare of those committed to my care." Desiring to make things better for others is part of the fabric of who I am. Of course, whether I actually make things better is debatable.

I want you, my reader, to feel good about yourself after you close the book. If you identify with some of my thoughts, emotions, and situations, I will feel satisfied. If I help you realize that it's ok to laugh at yourself, along with your imperfections, I will feel doubly satisfied.

We all want to feel normal. But really—what is normal? I'm sure everyone's definition is different. Learning to laugh at ourselves and find humor, even in the most upsetting of circumstances, is the best thing we can do for our psyches.

I Was Weird in First Grade

I sat in the last seat of Row 1, in a class of fifty-five children. Apparently I noticed the boys in first grade. One day I got called up to the teacher's desk to hand in a paper, and on the way, I stuck out my hand to pat the head of one surprised little boy named James, like he was a puppy dog. Why in the world do I remember this? There was no conversation between us. If by chance his wife reads my book, I can hear her saying, "Listen to this—how sweet!" And then—a flash of this strange memory will shoot through his subconscious.

Because I went to Catholic school, our three first grade reading groups had holy names. Not to brag, but I was in the top reading group, called the Blessed Mother group. The next level down was called the St Joseph group. And the students who struggled with reading belonged to the Guardian Angel group. Our groups would take turns and sit in chairs in front of the classroom to read aloud at the appointed time. I was not very nice to a certain classmate, when it was our turn to read. But to be fair, she wasn't very nice to me, either. We had the competition of the skirts. We sat next to each other, and the reading chairs were tightly placed; so when I sat down, I spread my pleated skirt out in a fan, over hers. Then Martha spread hers out over mine. This went on and on, until it was my turn to read aloud.

What can I say, except that I was weird in first grade.

Biting the Venetian Blinds

In 1953, my mother found a surprise on the front door Venetian blinds. A tiny set of teeth marks from four-year-old yours truly was left on one of the pliable aluminum slats. Temper tantrums were not tolerated in the fifties, so my only option was to stomp away and bite the blinds. Twenty years later, when I brought my future husband to meet my parents, I showed him those cute little teeth marks on the very same white Venetian blinds. The expression on his face was uneasy. Was he marrying a girl who bites when she's angry?

Another day as a teenager, when I was mad at my mother, I thought I successfully pulled off a Scarlett O'Hara. Storming up the steps to my bedroom, I slammed the door—picture frames vibrating on the walls—only to turn around five minutes later and see my mother standing in the doorway. By the way, she used to have a saying that only dogs get mad—people get angry. Not true.

As a sophomore in high school, my sister spilled the beans that my parents were planning a surprise sweet sixteen birthday party for me. Back in the sixties, we all gussied up for these parties and our first encounters with the boys. *My* big night finally arrived. I was led down our basement stairway, decorated with crepe paper and balloons to hear a roomful of girls scream, "Surprise!" Not one member of the opposite sex. Mom, what were you thinking? Don't worry—I managed to look elated.

I remember a pretty white dress she made for me to wear at a Holy Thursday procession in church. We processed up the center aisle in two rows, holding a basket of spring flowers; then stopped, turning to face each other, as we waited for the priest to walk past and up to the altar. According to my mother—while sitting in the pew, all she could see were the whites of my eyes, as my pupils darted back and forth. As an adult, I had surgery to tighten a muscle in my right

3

eye, which was causing occasional double vision. I often wonder if my nosy eyeballs were to blame.

My mother did her best to support my whims, and make them come true. I decided in fifth grade that I wanted to play the piano. I saw an ad in the local paper that someone was selling theirs on the other side of town. I have no idea how the two of us got over there, as we didn't yet own a car; but I remember going inside a house with an upright piano that we couldn't afford, much less the delivery charge. So instead of becoming the next Liberace (for my young readers, he was a pianist from the fifties), I decided to sing in the grade school talent shows.

The year before I got married, I watched the wedding of Luci Baines Johnson on TV. I was mesmerized by the Priscilla of Boston bridesmaids' veils, made of pink tulle that flowed breezily from their heads to the floor; and I wanted my mother to do the same for my bridesmaids. After many attempts, we ditched the idea. Shoulder length apricot colored veils, which sprouted from a big bow, was the final look.

I've realized it takes years to fully appreciate the efforts a mother goes through to make her children happy.

Living Vicariously

I went through a phase growing up with a goal to star on Broadway. If you read my first book, you'll remember how that went.

Around 1986, two of our four kids were still in elementary school. It was the year before I resumed my nursing career, after being a stay-at-home mom. I went to the school principal and offered to produce and direct a variety show.

Now, I didn't know how to read music, nor did I play an instrument. So I came up with this ingenious idea—transfer popular songs and show tunes to an old-fashioned tape recorder. The kids would sing along, and I'd kill two birds with one stone—the overall sound would be more professional, and my ignorance of musical notes, keys, and tempo wouldn't matter.

The kindergarten sang along to "Me and My Teddy Bear," wearing pajamas and holding their teddy bears. The first grade sang "How Much Is That Doggie in the Window?"—the kids all begging to be the lucky one to walk their puppy across the stage. The third grade belted out, "It's a Hard-Knock Life" from the musical, *Annie*. A cute little boy with a mighty voice screamed a solo line into the microphone, "TILL THIS DUMP SHINES LIKE THE TOP OF THE CHRYSLER BUILDING!"

The older grades sang a medley of songs: the Marlo Thomas children's hit, "Free To Be...You and Me", "I Won't Grow Up" from *Peter Pan*, "Let's Go Mets," and "Do-Re-Mi" from *The Sound of Music*.

According to my results on the Myers-Briggs personality test, I tend to make decisions based on feelings rather than facts, which is why those who auditioned for the acting parts put their names into a hat and I pulled out the winners. A Steven Spielberg I'll never be.

Considering the scope of what I took on, I considered myself lucky I had only one near disaster. Halfway through the show, the sound went dead. Without a backup piano player, I froze. I could hear whispers coming from the audience—oh, the humiliation! Within seconds, a teacher in the audience jumped up on stage, ran behind the curtains, and did something with the sound system (or maybe it was the tape recorder) to make the show come alive again. To this day, I don't know what he did.

And that was the end of my Broadway ambitions.

Transitioning to My Present Life

Those were my good old days. I have sprinklings of these earlier memories in the beginning of my first two books, as you remember—because you read them, right?

I still find it freaky when an old photo of our children pops up from out of nowhere, and I realize the bodies and minds of those little kids in the photo stretched and grew in slow motion over fifty years. As their mother, I still see the child in their faces.

Having adult children is the best. I no longer think of myself as a disciplinarian, and can enjoy watching them raise their own children. I give absolutely no advice unless asked. Impossible, you say? Well, I just stuff a handful of Lay's Kettle Cooked potato chips into my mouth to stop the urge to pontificate. I have a salty tooth. A cupcake might work better for you.

So—I will jump ahead to more present times.

The Green Monster

After making the disastrous mistake of buying an ultra-firm, expensive mattress which I thought would give good support to our aching backs, my husband Paul and I realized we would have saved a lot of money by just sleeping on the floor; so I took the advice of my friend and bought a mattress topper.

After researching them on the Internet, I ordered a four inch foam topper, the thickest I could find. It came in a square box, shrink wrapped in plastic. After I cut open the wrapper, I almost got a black eye, as a big green godzilla popped out. I'd better like it, I thought, because I sure as hell wasn't getting it back into the box. I could visualize the manufacturers laughing as they wrote, "Satisfaction guaranteed—returns gladly taken back."

Our mattress was high to begin with, so I already used a stool to climb into bed. And even though Paul is almost six feet tall, he also had a bit of trouble getting up onto the bed with its added four inches of foam, taking care not to strangle himself as he maneuvered the hose tethered to his BiPAP machine for sleep apnea. I found another stool in the basement—a Fisher Price relic from when the kids were little. "This will do the job," I said, as he climbed into bed. I held back the impulse to take a candid photo, which could come in handy someday, as blackmail on the family text thread.

A week later I proclaimed to Paul, "I feel like I'm getting sucked into quicksand." I have a fear of quicksand, although the only time I ever saw evidence of this scientific phenomena was in the old TV westerns of the 50s. I'd watch wide-eyed, as its victims screamed frantically.

One night I heard sirens closing in on the neighborhood. Enveloped in foam, jumping out of bed wasn't going to happen. I just lay there thinking, "Well, I don't smell smoke."

"We can't go on like this," I finally said to Paul. "It takes more energy than I can muster in the middle of the night to try and roll over on this thing." To which I got a reply, "Gee, my back has never felt better."

A friend of mine suggested satin sheets. "They have a slippery feel, so maybe you could maneuver in the bed better. Just don't buy satin pajamas, too. You might propel yourself across the room."

Four inches of foam was beginning to affect our relationship. One morning, I ripped the green monster off the bed, dragged it into the guest room, rolled it up as the corners wacked me in the face, and shoved it into the closet. If the guest room bed is the new recipient of the green monster, I do believe we'll never have another guest overstay their welcome.

The TV, Paul, and Me

Paul gets up an hour before me in the morning. He's very quiet, unless he's running late to meet up with his golf buddies. I pretend I'm asleep so I don't have to talk, as he is closing drawers and doors, flushing and flossing. I just pull my blankets up tighter and fall asleep again before he even gets out of the garage.

Next thing I knew, one morning—it was ten o'clock. It must have been the melatonin I took the night before. I pull a ten o'clocker about twice a year. When this happens, it feels so good and clears out my brain. I make myself a cup of coffee and sit in peace and quiet, to spend a few moments thinking and praying. The prayer part is actually a litany of urgent requests, which has multiplied exponentially since our four children got married and had their own kids.

But back to Paul—on his non-golfing days we both sit in our recliners wearing our bathrobes, watching the news while checking Facebook, email, and the weather on our phones. One of our kids once proclaimed, "You're worse than our teenagers, with your heads stuck in your phones."

"Don't be so hard on us. It helps us feel grounded, before we start our day. And besides, we also look up once in a while to catch an interesting clip on cable news. Your father enjoys debating all the controversial topics with me." Do we disagree? All the time.

With the exception of the season playoffs in football, basketball, and baseball—I'm not a play-by-play TV sports fan. Paul must think I am, as he comments on the merits of each play. That's ok. I just feel bad that I have no coherent answers for him. And you can only say, "Wow" or "Oh, right" so many times.

We both got hooked on Netflix during the pandemic. I learned a lot and I'm willing to share my knowledge. I do believe I could tame a wild horse (*Heartland*), deliver a baby (*Call the Midwife*), and use proper British etiquette (*The Crown*). I'm happy to give you a crash course in case you are invited to tea at Buckingham Palace.

The Grandcats

You might remember the saga of Misty, the kitten that wandered into our yard from my first book. It was our one and only pet, and that was by default. Our four grown kids now own dogs. And one of them owns not only a dog, but two cats. As a result of all our visits, I am becoming an expert on felines and canines. I've come a long way. I used to say I only loved these furry pets on birthday cards.

I have found that dogs are easier to figure out than cats, which are a little like my girls growing up. You're never quite sure what's going on in their little brains.

Eleanor, one of our daughters, has the two cats—Costello and Lucky. Costello is a happy cat with soft, blond fur who climbs up on the sofa to purr and bump his head into me—and he talks! Cat language, of course. Costello meows every time I talk to him. I end up saying meow back, as it seems polite.

Lucky is another story. This black cat was the runt of a litter from a feral cat who gave birth under El's porch. Little baby Lucky was abandoned by his mother. Eleanor brought him into the house, made a soft little bed in a shoebox, and fed Lucky with a dropper, while holding him in the palm of her hand. On one visit, I even took turns massaging the little kitty's belly, stimulating him to poop and pee.

I got no thanks from Lucky for being an integral part of his life. He now tolerates me near him, but if I head in his direction, Lucky darts through narrow passages to avoid me. And the topping on the cake is when this little orphan cat hisses at me when I try to pet him.

"Mom, don't look so scared. He can sense that. And whenever you talk to him, your voice goes up two octaves. That sounds freaky even to me!"

"El, I'm fine with us both keeping a polite distance." I have a theory. My voice isn't exactly soft. In fact, I hate hearing myself in a video. Also, I move fast. I really think he's afraid.

After a few years of our polite, human/cat relationship, while living together under the same roof on our visits, I thought he might be warming up. I knew he was capable of being lovey, as he is always snuggling up to Eleanor and the rest of the family in the evenings. Just be patient, I thought.

And then—I was reaching into their kitchen cabinet to pull out a box of pasta, when I lost my balance and tripped backwards into the chair where he was curled up in a ball. Startled, Lucky jumped four feet into the air, hissed, and darted down to the basement.

I started googling cat behavior when we got home. Because of the computer spies, I am now bombarded with all things psychological related to cats. And the worst part is that I have to read them. I can't help it. So feel free to call me if you are having any issues with your kitty.

The Gloves

Have you noticed that during our doctor's visits we are rarely asked to disrobe and put on a paper gown, like in the old days? Back then, it didn't matter if they were diagnosing a broken arm. After all, you might also have an appendix about to rupture. However, assessing the total patient was mostly a good thing.

With a dearth of doctors in many areas, I know they need to squeeze in more visits; and anyone who dresses and undresses as slow as I (leaning on anything upright to keep from falling), is a big time waster. Besides, all the diagnostic imaging available these days allows them to see the tiniest of organs, while poking and prodding can be done through a layer of fabric.

Of course, going to the gyn doctor is a different story, for obvious reasons. I had a good gyn doctor years ago who was also a very good conversationalist. I made the mistake of asking him a question as he was about to do the pelvic exam, to combat the awkwardness.

"Have you ever seen the Broadway show, Annie?"

He had just donned his examining gloves, and stopped what he was doing to answer my question. "Oh yes, my wife and I saw it about six months ago. I particularly liked..."

My ears didn't hear a word he said. No, my eyes just followed him placing his *gloved* hands on his hips while he talked. Now I realize this wasn't the operating room, where everything must be sterile, but still—not a good visual in the brain of someone with OCD.

And, I've learned to save my questions for strategic times in doctor visits for another reason. I don't want to distract them while they are looking for red flags during an exam. I'm sure if they graduated from Harvard, they can do two things at one time, but I'm not taking any chances.

After a recent visit with Paul to his cardiologist, I said, back in the car, "Didn't you see me giving you the eye in there?"

"Yes, and I was wondering why you were winking at me."

"I wasn't winking. You were going on and on about your golf game, and distracting him from your AFib episodes."

"You ask too many questions. He thinks I'm fine."

"Because you told him you got a birdie on the ninth hole yesterday?"

The Faceplant

I know you're tired of my tripping and falling stories, but this was the mother of all falls, so I need to tell you.

One winter day, while on a walk in my neighborhood, I saw a rescue squad barreling down the street. As it began to turn left up ahead, the nurse in me wondered—heart attack, insulin shock, stroke? I picked up the pace, as I saw them carry a stretcher into the house.

And then—I stubbed my toe on the sidewalk, and because of my bulky down coat—did not get my arms out in front of me in time, as I faceplanted.

The next thing I heard was a crunch in my mouth, and as I lifted my head, saw blood dripping. When I realized I didn't pass out, I jumped up as quickly as I fell. My vanity always supersedes my catastrophes. I started to walk fast (repeating my mistake), with my gloved hand covering my mouth. No Hansel and Gretel red bread-crumbs would be left by me.

I called Paul on my cell with my free hand who, thank God, was turning the corner on his way home from the gym. And off we went to our hospital's ER. It was in the middle of COVID, and I wanted Paul to drop me off, but he insisted on staying by my side.

Two hours later, I had six stitches in my lip. I know this isn't very funny yet, so how can I break this up? Let's see—oh, my bladder was about to burst, but using an ER bathroom during COVID gave me the creeps. I really had no choice, so I went in and made my usual bird's nest of toilet paper before sitting. My hips won't let me hover anymore.

Anyway, I got back to the room just in time for my discharge instructions and then got dressed to leave. I started to walk past Paul, only to hear him say, "What's that hanging from your waist?"

A part of my bird's nest of toilet paper was trailing from my waist to the floor—so gross!

I visited the dentist the next day. He had that serious look I never like to see on a provider's face and told me he couldn't save one of the teeth that had a confrontation with concrete. So, off to the oral surgeon.

I would need an implant (aka fake tooth). This was all new to me, and I didn't realize I wasn't going home with a brand new tooth the same day. In fact, all I was getting was a screw into the bone where my old tooth used to be.

"Yes, in about four months or so, you'll look like your old self," said the oral surgeon, with a smile.

"Four months? You're joking, right?"

"No, I am not. It takes that long for your bone to fuse with the screw. We are giving you a plastic retainer that has a temporary tooth. It will be your companion for the next few months, and you can take it out whenever you want."

When we got home that evening, I popped the fake tooth out, rinsed my mouth, and looked in the mirror. "Oh my God, I can't see the screw! Did I just spit it down the drain?"

In a panic, I called the office. "I just had an implant screw put in two hours ago. I know your office closes in five minutes, but will you please tell the oral surgeon I can't see the screw?"

He called back shortly after, having a hard time believing I was a nurse, and said the screw was in tightly and wouldn't come out. And sure enough, after rinsing a few more times, a glint of silver peaked back at me.

Off we went to Florida a few weeks later, taking special care not to lose my plastic retainer. It was tricky to eat with it in, so since it was 2021 and we wore masks going out, I just left the retainer in its case most of the time, putting up with Paul calling me Hillbilly Sally at home. The whole thing was a humbling experience. I showed up at the condo swimming pool one day, where we weren't required to wear masks. Forgetting to put my retainer with the temporary tooth in my mouth, I gave a big smile to everyone, as they all did a double take.

I welcomed my new tooth with open arms when it was finally ready. The dentist's assistant was very fastidious about matching the other teeth, and presented a tray full of different shades. I picked a bright white, but she pointed out that wasn't a good choice, as my teeth were a dull ivory. Anyway, on the day I smiled into a mirror with my new tooth in place, my dentist was ecstatic for me. He reminded me of my obstetricians and their reactions after they just delivered my babies.

I finally moved on. Although, now when I go for a walk, I whisper to myself, "Heel-toe, heel-toe."

My First Uber Ride

I was vacationing in Florida with Paul and had to fly to Baltimore, as my mother was in the hospital. I told Sharon, our oldest daughter, that I would take a cab from the airport.

"A cab? Mom, take an Uber. It's so easy." She told me how to use the Uber app on my iPhone, and instructed, "Don't call the Uber until you retrieve your checked baggage; then make a note of which numbered door you're standing under."

So after we landed, I got my bags, proceeded to door #4, and hit the Uber app on my phone. "Where do you want to go, and at what door are you waiting?" popped up on the screen. I typed in the address of the hospital and door #4. So far so good. Then up popped a notation that a black Kia would show up at door #4 in five minutes.

Oh great, I thought. I don't know one car from another. And it's black? Why couldn't it be orange? I walked out door #4 with a crowd of other people where it was dark, under an overpass. I had a sick feeling in my stomach, and started to feel like a dope. My phone beeped with another message—"Hi, this is John. I am approaching door #4 in a black Kia."

I texted back, "I am here, but I don't know what a Kia looks like. Just look for me—I'm wearing a black coat." (Like 70 percent of everyone else.)

All of a sudden I saw a hand raised in the air, looking straight at me. I guess he was used to first timers. "Oh thank God!" I walked towards the black *whatever it was,* remembering I was supposed to verify the license plate before getting in the car. Well, too late for that. The trunk was already popped open. I was so rattled by this time, and even though I don't know my cars, I recognized his face from the Uber app. So, off we went!

I've had some pretty interesting Uber drivers. I asked one what country he was from, getting nervous after I asked, because of the political climate regarding immigrants. He said, "Ethiopia," and my mind went into first gear.

"Wasn't Haile Selassie the emperor of Ethiopia up until the 1970s?" I piqued his interest, and I was on a roll. I told him I just finished a book called *Cutting for Stone*, which took place in Ethiopia. And then he told me his own story. I love hearing other people's stories—kind of like reading a book.

The best part of Uber riding is I don't have to anticipate the fare or dig around in my purse for money.

Passwords, Cookies and CAPTCHA

I've always had a love-hate relationship with computers. Back in the days when I worked as an RN in acute care hospitals, paper charting (yes—that's how old I am) eventually switched to computer charting. Computers slowed down my documentation. Having learned the Palmer method of penmanship, I'm a really fast scribbler, and I resented having to enter my nursing password and click through three computer screens in order to get to the right patient just to say that he peed.

Passwords are the downside of innovation, I suppose. I thought I outsmarted Bill Gates by implementing a Pentagon level of quirky passwords, only to have the system fail when I hid the passwords in an empty box of pasta (for security) and Paul threw it in the recycling.

After trying desperately to reset my passwords, I found the computer wants to make sure I'm really me, starting with security questions I must have answered a year ago. No problem—what food did I hate as a child? Glad for the easy question—I typed in liver. The big red letters popped up saying "Wrong."

My computer rage rose to the surface yet again. The only food I ever gagged on as a kid was liver—maybe because my mother fried it too long and it turned into leather; but that's beside the point. Liver was the only possible answer.

The Captcha authentication step that wants to make sure I'm a human makes me very nervous. You know—those squares that ask you to put a check on all the images with a boat, or a stop light, etc. It's like a former teacher is going to jump out of the computer screen, or a psychiatrist is giving me some sort of Rorschach test. And that freaky question—asking if I'm a robot. I want to give a sarcastic answer, but they only give you a little box to check.

I recently had to ask Google what it meant to accept "cookies" when I opened up an Internet site. I'm embarrassed to say I always clicked yes, without having any idea whether they were Toll House cookies for the robot or me. After reading the Google explanation, I figured it was OK to accept them—something about improving my web browsing experience. We can trust Google, right? I got more intimidated the more I read about cookies on the Internet, so I stopped reading. Up until now, all I worried about was whether my computer would get indigestion from all the Oreos I was feeding it.

I Dropped the Ball This Year

As Christmas approached last year—to send or not to send cards. "Damn, the Smiths sent us a card again this year," I said to Paul. "And I already crossed them off our list."

"Well, that's because you tried to cross them off our list last year, and when they sent one to us, you scrambled to get a card in the mail. You've created a vicious cycle."

"I don't like the way you said that. The Christmas spirit shouldn't be vicious."

"It's very simple. Don't send a card back. Lots of people are switching to Facebook greetings, anyway."

Okay—something to think about. But for this year, the challenge of the card. It wouldn't be a challenge if I had the foresight to corral the family the last time we were all together, for a picture—forget attempting the matching khaki and blue outfits at the beach. In my previous book, I described my journey from hand written notes inside the cards to amateur photocopies of the kids along with their ages scribbled in; finally realizing there were photo companies out there who could do the whole thing for a price—so I got smart and moved into the 21st century.

And that is why I felt like a fraud this year—running to Walmart to scrounge up the last few boxes of Christmas and holiday cards that remained on the shelves. I dropped the ball this time. Of course, barely surviving 2021 COVID issues could be my excuse. If we didn't move to so many places over the years, I wouldn't have to reach out and touch so many friends with our updates and photos.

I never saw the point of just sending a card with only a signature to someone that you haven't seen in years; so to preserve some credibility, I decided to type a few sentences on the computer. Not a typical holiday letter—bragging that a grandchild attained her Masters in chemical engineering at the age of 11. No, it was more like an explanation of why they got a typed, five sentence insert.

Also—I never took the time to learn how to print out address labels on the computer; and it didn't seem right to use the *return* address labels sent from St Jude's Children's Hospital if I didn't contribute. So, everything on the envelope was handwritten.

"You've got to help me this year, Paul. You've got 30 nieces and nephews on your side. He really got into it, I must say—though I happened to see the third card, looking over his shoulder.

"This is your niece, Paul. Why did you sign it "Paul and Mary Ann Hoyt"?

"Oh, right. Well—I'm not redoing it."

Addendum: Less than three months after an interstate move (which I will tell you about later), Christmas and the holidays descended on us early. So needless to say, I was down to the wire again, minus a family photo. But, I had the perfect solution.

"Paul, we are not chopping our list this year, or nobody will know we moved." It was actually easy—a selfie of Paul and me in front of our new home, with copies ordered online. Bam!

New Year's resolution: make a contribution to St Jude's this year—and get the family picture. I have 365 days left.

Masks, Make-up and Smiles

I read that as we get older, our skin thins out and no longer hides what's underneath, like the tiny blood vessels that give us those dark circles under the eyes.

Now I know why, the older we get, the more we treasure staring into a baby's perfect face, with their smooth, ivory skin, their pink rosebud lips—always surrounded by the faint scent of baby powder. Maternal instincts aside, we are living vicariously for a brief interlude. And then it hits me that I'm no longer a spring tulip, but rather, an autumn chrysanthemum, dropping its petals—fast.

Some faces have a natural beauty as they age, but mine needs a little help. I don't mind a few wrinkles, but without lipstick, I look either mad or sick. So I make no apologies to the naturalists out there for my attempts to look happy and healthy. I saved a ton of lipstick money during the two years we wore face coverings. I had concern during one of my book signings where I had to wear a mask. How would anyone know I was smiling?—an interaction so important at a book signing. So I googled for some tips and, apparently it's all in the eyes. When you smile, your eyes squint a bit.

Unfortunately, I spent the pandemic lipstick savings on eye makeup. At 74, I am still aiming for Bette Davis eyes.

The older I got, eyeliner became a challenge to apply, as my eyelids wiggle too much. After I'd fix my mistakes, I looked like I was ready to go trick-or-treating. Such freedom I felt, as I threw my eyeliner into the trash.

Mascara has always been a bit of a challenge, too. Every time I think I've applied the right one, a daughter of mine will say, "Mom, you need to use some mascara." My latest purchase was a brand I got online. It seems to form little tubes around the lashes, and is definitely the best so far. One night I forgot to wash it off and the next morning I scared the heck out of Paul. "What happened to your face?

You've got long black lines running down your cheeks! You look like Frankenstein's mother."

I was in the bathroom at one of our granddaughters recently and saw what I thought was an eyelash curler. "Do these things really work?" I asked her.

"Yes, Grandma, it makes your lashes curl up and look longer."

I bought one of these intimidating gadgets and told Paul he was about to see a transformation. I looked up close into the bathroom mirror, realizing I couldn't use my reading glasses and manipulate the eyelash curler at the same time; and all I could see was a blurry vision of an eyeball—forget the lashes. I gingerly placed the curler at what I hoped was the base of my left eye's top lashes and closed it gently for twenty seconds. When I released it, I saw nothing that warranted my four dollar purchase.

What nobody told me was that you need half decent lashes to work with. And I'm certainly not doing the false eyelash thing. My mascara will be good enough. In fact, I say that about a lot of things these days. Enough.

Enough—except for my neck. I'd love to find a plastic surgeon who will do an under the chin tuck for the same price I pay to get my teeth cleaned. What good are white teeth if everyone's gaze drifts down to a turkey neck. I know, in today's world, this is not only trivial, but selfish to obsess over, but how difficult can it be to tack a string on either side of my neck and hike it up under my chin?

Maybe I could get our son, Brian, to look into it. I remember, when he was ten years old, he came out of the bathroom holding the Readers' Digest, and told me he just learned how to do brain surgery. "Really, Mom, I think I could do it if I had to!"

Tornado Warning

I always associated tornadoes with Dorothy, the wicked witch, and Kansas. A few years ago, our cell phones started screeching in our Delaware home—a tornado *watch*? No, it was the more serious *warning*. I knew we had to go straight to the basement. What I didn't think to do was to pee first, and then throw some cheese and crackers into a bag along with a bottle of wine.

Our basement is cold and unfinished, with two old desk chairs the only furniture next to the Christmas decorations, tools and random basement stuff.

Anyway, Paul and I sat face to face, staring at each other and monitoring our phones. This was all new to us. Every time we got near the *all clear* notice, within seconds a new alarm popped up with a warning that a new tornado was forming from another direction.

After an hour and a half of staring at each other and our phones, I said, "This is ridiculous. I'm taking my life in my hands and running upstairs for that bottle of wine."

"Keep in mind we don't have a bathroom down here."

I pointed to the commode in the corner of the basement, from when my elderly mother stayed with us. "I knew that would come in handy someday."

My Responsibility to the Grandchildren

How could I let our grandchildren go off to college without relating what could have been a disaster when I was their age. Yes, I decided to swallow my pride and fall off my grandma pedestal for the greater good.

I went to a Catholic nursing school in the 60s, one step away from a convent. One evening, I went with a few friends to a party at a nearby college. I was very naïve. Nobody ever warned me about the punch.

We entered the room, trying to look like sophisticated party girls and I saw this enormous bowl of grape punch. A handsome guy was only too willing to give me a glass of the most delicious grape juice I ever tasted. I had another.

God only knows what else was in that punch. I only remember going into a bigger room with my friends and started dancing to a band playing 60s music—for maybe thirty seconds. Then something weird happened. Everybody and everything I looked at started swaying.

I bet this is what it feels like to be drunk, I thought. I sat down on a chair until I had an overwhelming feeling of nausea. I knew instantly that I had only minutes before I would have projectile vomiting, so I jumped up and asked a college boy where the bathroom was.

I was pointed to a stairwell that went up to the second floor. And instead of going outside, I stupidly headed upstairs. I had trouble getting up the steps, and as I was crawling up on all fours, I felt someone giving my butt a few shoves to help me get to the top.

Surprisingly, I only had dry heaves in a very disgusting bathroom and soon, miraculously, made it back to my nursing school dorm. So that the housemother would not suspect anything amiss, instead of signing in at her desk by the front entrance, we came through the back door, where we called out to her—smiling and giving her a big wave.

The next thing I knew, it was morning. I woke up with a Rolaids tablet still undissolved on my dry tongue. Boy—I was so lucky that night.

You should have seen my granddaughters' eyeballs during that story. I hope they recovered from the visual lesson I tried to give them. Beware of the punch.

Take Off Your Reading Glasses Unless You Are Reading

I was bringing a few boxes to The UPS Store for Amazon returns. I got out of the car, and while balancing the boxes, took out my phone and reading glasses so I could have the emails ready with the QR codes. I slammed the car door shut with my foot and proceeded to the store. I realized I put my glasses on prematurely, so everything was a tad blurry, but I only had a few yards to walk. I caught up to the lady in front of me, so close that she had no choice but to hold the door open for me.

I saw the clerk at the front counter eye me with a quizzical look.

"Sorry, but your frames didn't come in yet," she said to the customer in front of me.

That's odd, I thought, simultaneously seeing rows of frames on the side wall.

"Oh damn, I'm in Vision World!"

I made an about face, before I had to say anything. Kind of like the same reaction I exhibit after I fall—righting myself into a vertical position in half a second and raising my hand to any startled spectators, saying "I'm good."

I was telling my sister, Betsy, on the way home. "Why didn't you take your reading glasses off before you walked over to the store?" she asked.

"And why are you asking me such a logical question?"

The Jet Skis

I traveled to Fort Lauderdale by air with our youngest daughter, Annie, recently for a funeral. I realized quickly that Paul had prepped her. I could hear his voice in my head. "You gotta watch over your mother." Every time we neared a crack in the sidewalk or a curb, I felt Annie's hand on my elbow, with gentle alerts.

"Please stop touching me!" I said. "It makes me feel like I'm a hundred years old." I kind of get it, considering the periodic phone calls they've gotten regarding my inability to remain erect.

Speaking of feeling old, being around our kids shows us how our lifestyle has changed. And it's not like we are couch potatoes. In fact, Paul spends so much time at the gym, they really ought to put his photo on a wall at the Y. But in comparison, our kids are on Pelotons at 5:30 a.m., before they go to work. When they go to the beach, they leave early after packing lunches, and come home whenever. In comparison, we take two hours to fully wake up in the morning, make sure our GI systems are working after our morning coffee and toast; and then we go to the beach for two hours in the late afternoon. "You get a better parking space," Paul explained to them, "if you go at 3 p.m. when people are leaving."

One of our kids got Jet Skis for their family. I don't have an adventurous bone in my body, so even though they've asked me to hop on with them, I know they were just being polite. The follow-up question was, "How about you and Dad drive over to the Rusty Rudder Restaurant and we'll jet-ski over to meet you." I liked that option.

Their nightlife exhausts me—and this is just from checking out the late night times they posted pictures on Facebook.

Sometimes our family text thread starts chiming rapid fire at 10 p.m. I hear a guttural voice through a BiPAP mask say, "Dammit, don't they know what time it is?"

"Well, my dear, you forgot to turn off your phone."

"What did they want?" he comes back with—a mix of fearing the worst and curiosity.

Paul usually falls asleep before me, so I turn the sound off on my iPhone, while I'm reading my Kindle in bed, though out of the corner of my eye I can see what looks like lightening, as the messages flash on and off, (which I can't *not* look at either).

The sound on my phone goes back on before I finally close my eyes in case well, you know…

My Big Handbag

I thought my new handbag was perfect. It had at least eight zippered enclosures and pockets. My need for organization found its match—until I realized my brain remembers nothing anymore. It became a frustrating guessing game.

Parked in the Lowe's parking lot, Paul asked, "Do you have a pen, Mary Ann?"

"Hang on while I get it out. Here's your—oh wait, this is the lipstick pocket. Give me a second."

"Forget it. I found one in the console."

So I gave that handbag to charity and spent $13 at Walmart for one that feels expensive because of its soft leather, but looks like a feed bag that hangs around a horse's neck. And I do just as much swearing as I dig into the bottomless pit as I did with all the pockets and zippers. Lord only knows what's buried in the depths of this thing. In fact, every couple months, I dump the contents onto the kitchen table—five pens, three Purells, a cheese stick…

And this is why I ditch the handbag and use the pockets in my jeans for short trips to the grocery store.

How My Miscarriage Led to a Scribbled Will

Have you ever had a miscarriage? It's sad to get your hopes up for two months and then—within just a few hours, you've lost the baby for whom you already picked a name. The fact that it would have been baby number five made no difference to me. I remember explaining to our kids that a miscarriage is a little like planting a few seeds in your flower garden. Sometimes a seed just doesn't sprout.

Paul was at an out-of-state business conference when the cramping started. I had an inkling of what was happening, so I got a babysitter for our kids and asked my friend to drive me to the hospital.

As with anything bad or sad, I can eventually find something to smile about. Lying in the hospital bed, I realized we had no will. If Paul's plane went down on the way home, and I had a bad outcome (both highly unlikely), we had four kids with no place to go.

So I asked someone from the hospital, who was a notary, to come and witness my hastily scribbled directions, written on the back of a check, instructing that our four children be left with my mother. This was when my mother was around 60—really brazen of me to hand off our children without even asking. Paul and I both survived, and we finally got around to making a formal will. We are really slackers when it comes to this kind of thing.

Our first revision didn't come until my mother was 90, living in assisted living. Would you believe the assisted living facility told me they couldn't accommodate our two younger kids? So back to the lawyer.

My Extreme Distaste for Sewing

One of the happiest days of my life was the day I gave my portable sewing machine to Goodwill. I liked sewing as much as I liked sailing, and if you read my first book, you know how that went.

Soon after we were married, in 1970, Paul showed me a hole in his sock. He suggested we get darning tools—one of those wooden darning eggs and a thick needle. He told me proudly that his father taught him how to darn.

"Well, I think you should keep up the tradition!" Of course, he never darned his sock. It disappeared from his sock drawer when he realized Mrs Betty Crocker wasn't going to do it either.

Over the years, I've done everything I could do to avoid sewing—iron-on tape to repair a hem and safety pins for anything else. Although, I did repair the canvas strap of Paul's backpack that he took to the beach. The repair held, but it was a major fail. As he stuffed a towel into his backpack, I heard him yell "Ow!" He held up a bloody finger, sporting a deep puncture wound from the needle I forgot to cut loose from the thread.

In over 50 years of marriage, I've saved hundreds of old buttons in case I could match one to a piece of clothing missing a button. That's what we were taught, right? I probably went into my button box a total of five times. So, I finally gave my orphan buttons to someone who genuinely appreciated them. Eleanor, our daughter, has given them a place in her multi-media artwork. Along with the scraps of metal and fabric she uses, the images are then covered with oil paints. The resulting scenes of New York City and New Orleans never looked so grand. And I'm happy my lonely, discarded buttons have come to a better fate than a box hidden in the depths of my closet.

Running a Red Light

It happened one sunny afternoon, driving home on a busy street. I wasn't on my phone, but my mind was obviously somewhere else, when I realized I was driving through a red light, with two cars swerving to miss me.

If you ever ran a red light, you know how traumatic it is. And if you ever ran a red light and almost hit another car, or two, you have to know that my Catholic guilt and PTSD were overwhelming. I thank God no one was hurt, but it upset me just the same.

The one that barely missed me made the turn and was now behind me. Holy crap—every muscle in my body was trembling and my mind was now spiraling. What do I do now? I didn't hit them, so it's not a hit and run if I don't stop. But, am I supposed to stop and apologize?

As I drove at a snail's pace, I noticed in the rear view mirror that there were two in the front seat. Great, one probably took down my license plate and already called the police. I figured a patrol car was waiting for me at the next light.

After about five miles, she turned off the road. Hmm, what did that mean? A mile later I turned into a CVS parking lot and called my brother, the lawyer. He was no help as his expertise was corporate finance. He googled stuff about citizen arrests and running traffic lights and how each state had its own rules.

"Oh, how am I going to tell Paul?"

"Well, you might not have to if a policeman beats you home."

No one showed up at my front door, and I never got a summons in the mail. I eventually calmed down, despite the meme of a swat team showing up at my house, which was sent to my text. Thanks a lot, brother.

I learned my lesson—again. Focus, focus. I am so lucky no one got hurt, or worse. And my new prayer is, "Please God, keep our children and grandchildren safe at the wheel."

It's All About the Core

I had some big time physical therapy for my hips and back, with the hope I would strengthen my core. Everything's about the core. My kids won't shut up about it. Every time I have a muscular skeletal complaint, I hear, "Mom, you've got to do something about your core."

My primary doctor agreed, after she reviewed the results of my x-rays.

"Well, first I have to buy some physical therapy clothes," I said to my daughter.

"Physical therapy clothes?"

"Yes, you know—like tights and tops that cover my butt."

"First of all, Mom—they are not called tights. You're not going to ballet class. They're called leggings or yoga pants." When I got to my PT visits, I could pick out the ladies who didn't have daughters advising them.

By the way, the PT stretches and exercises have made a big difference. I even packed my two inch foam floor mat into the car so I could work on my core while on vacation in Florida.

Manicures

I can't be trusted with manicures. Two hours after I'm home, my nails look like I was in a cat fight. "You need gel nails, Mom," said one of our daughters. "They're indestructible." So on vacation, I made my girls proud and got my first gel manicure.

"I thought you told me gel nails don't chip!" I said to one of them two days later.

"They don't. What were you doing?"

"Well, you said they were strong, so I gave my Brillo pad a little help in cleaning a roasting pan."

"Mom! Get rubber gloves, or just line the pan with aluminum foil."

"Yes, I could do both. I forgot, just like I always forget to put on garden gloves when I start yanking out weeds. I'm sorry, but I just can't be a slave to my nails. Don't worry, though. I'll sign up to get my nails done when I'm in assisted living. When your Grandma was there, I remember the volunteers painting all the residents' nails."

Now, pedicures—that's a different story. I don't even need the gel polish. The regular works just fine. I obviously take better care of my feet than my hands.

Airports and the TSA

The last time I flew on an airplane, I took an economy airline, where I had to pay for my checked bags, and an additional fee if they were over forty pounds. I stuffed a week's worth of clothes, shoes, and a makeup bag into my suitcase. It felt like it weighed a ton when I tried to lift it—eighty pounds for sure. So I rolled it into the bathroom, and hoisted it onto the bathroom scale. Twenty-nine pounds? Impossible. I made Paul come in and check the scale. The scale was right. Of course, our kids found this all quite humorous.

The next week, one of our granddaughters who was flying back to college had to pay a whopping surcharge because her luggage was over the weight limit. Hmm, I guess she didn't use the bathroom scale.

By the way, I still don't know why I got a pat down, the last time I flew. I was sure I had everything covered—no belt, no jewelry. I had perfect behavior, smiling and thanking all the TSA personnel. Maybe my niceness looked suspicious. Or maybe it was the face I made when I had to put my shoes, jacket, and handbag into those nasty checkpoint plastic bins.

I really wish I knew for the next time. I never asked what set the alarm off. I always get so rattled—feeling like a criminal, as I watch the bin with my shoes, handbag and jacket disappear in front of me on the conveyor belt. And I don't dare tell the TSA employee to hurry up with her pat down. No wonder the bars do a big business on the other side of security.

I just thought of something. Maybe I'm on *The List,* because of an incident at an airport a few years back. We were dropping a daughter off at a small rural airport and when I got back to the car, I realized she forgot her phone charger. "Oh damn it, Paul. Wait in the car and I will run it in to her." So I charged into this small airport toward security and I could see her in the line that was snaking to the scanners.

"Eleanor!" I yelled. As she turned to look at me, I was about to heave the charger cord over two rows of passengers when a TSA employee snatched it from my hand saying, "I'll take that." Oops.

"Sorry, Ma'am. I really wasn't thinking."

Bowls—Salad of the 2020s

While visiting our kids in Rhode Island, I asked a granddaughter at a cute little café, "What would you like for lunch, honey? I see they have Reuben sandwiches and salads and pizza."

"Oh Grandma, I think I will have a bowl."

"A bowl of what—soup?"

"No, I'm getting a cauliflower bowl with chick peas and quinoa." Her bowl came out with the chick peas and cauliflower artistically arranged on top of the quinoa with something red drizzled over the top.

"What's that?" I asked. "Oh, it's an Asian chili sauce with garlic to add color and flavor." I wanted her to know I was interested in her life, so the next day I told her I googled *bowls*.

"You googled bowls?" she laughed.

"Yes, and did you know there are so many different types? Smoothie bowls, Buddha bowls, poke bowls, power bowls..." Not sure she was impressed. She's probably tried them all.

I think it's actually a gimmick. Next time you have guests for dinner, just dump the salad in a bowl and drizzle something on top. Your guests will be impressed. Although, if they are my age, they'll still call it a salad.

When we got back home to Delaware, Paul asked what was for dinner. "A surprise," I said. Food surprises make him nervous. I chopped up a rotisserie chicken, dumped it in a bowl with a bunch of leftover peas, wild rice, and a few nuts for good measure. A dollop of spicy mayonnaise graced the top with a sprinkle of paprika for color.

"This is your *Leftovers with Love* bowl, honey!"

My Vanity

At a family picnic many years ago, someone took photos of all the cousins in my grandparents' back yard. After the group picture, I yelled, "Wait, can you take one of just me?" For some reason, I still had on my Sunday dress, and I plopped my ten-year-old frame onto the grass in front of a red rose bush, and took on an Audrey Hepburn expression. Looking at this 3x5 black and white photo years later, I would say my attempt at a pensive, far away expression looked more like a big pout.

Sadly, the caption under my picture from our nursing school year-book was, "Do I look all right?" I think some of this is genetic. Even though my mother didn't wear a lot of make-up, she always applied her lipstick before my Dad got home from work—Revlon's *Cherries in the Snow.* Years later at the assisted living facility, when she was finished combing her hair, she would hand me the comb and ask me to check the back, to make sure that none of her scalp showed through her salt and pepper hair. I guess she didn't realize that she was blessed with a thick mane of hair till the day she died.

I remember being wheeled into the holding area of the OR prior to my hysterectomy, where the anesthesiologist came out to meet me. After taking one look at my fly away hair, as I clutched the paper head covering in my hands, he said, "You do know you have to put that on your head before you have surgery."

"Of course I know. I was just waiting until all the introductions were over."

My Pet Sitting Skills Are Lacking

You all know, if you read my first two books, that my pet sitting is hit or miss. Our last fiasco was staying with a granddaughter while her mom and dad were at Parents' Weekend for her sibling in college.

Duke, their big dog, was well behaved and docile. The two cats were too, except for their escape gene. Especially Lucky, the black cat who sensed a half opened door from an upstairs bedroom. One night they both escaped. Oh crap—El and Craig are coming home to two dead cats. I went from door to door, meowing into the night. Finally, one of them came prancing back around midnight, but I was too tired to wait up for the second. Around 5 a.m., I heard meowing in my torturous dreams. I got up to go to the bathroom, and realized the meowing was outside the front door. He ran past me into the house without even a thank you glance.

Duke, the dog, only gave me a problem once. El and Craig were coming home that evening, so I washed all the linens on their bed, including the white quilt. I was in the basement unloading a dryer full of clothes when I heard a commotion with loud thuds on the floorboards right above me. And a minute later—"Mary Ann, you better come up now!" yelled Paul.

Black paw prints from the damp mulch outside were now all over the white quilt on the bed. Our granddaughter volunteered, "Sometimes he gets a little crazy after sprinting around the back yard. After he comes back in the house, he acts like an excited puppy for about ten minutes." Right—an excited puppy who just gave me more work to do.

So back to the basement with the quilt and stain remover tucked under my arm.

"How'd you do with the pets?" asked Eleanor on their return.

"They are alive and all accounted for—which I couldn't say a day ago."

Pickleball in Florida

We had a good time in Florida this year, catching up with friends we missed during the pandemic. Pickleball was really big down there this year, for the players and those who think they are pickleball players. "Are you going to play?" asked a friend.

"You're joking, right? I can't walk without tripping on a crack in the sidewalk."

Paul, on the other hand, can play any sport he likes with a degree of proficiency. It's maddening. He's also very competitive, which is evident on the pickleball courts.

"Oh, we just play for fun," they all say. Don't believe it. Pickleball is serious stuff. One young and very fit guy told us he got slammed by an eighty-year-old woman. He was also impressed with the plethora of colorful language coming out of the mouths of some proper looking, over-seventy ladies.

I left my mark last year on Florida's environment and pristine waters, sorrowfully. I was out for a walk one morning on the decks along the canal, and stopped to look for dolphins or a manatee. As I leaned over the railing, I dropped my empty plastic water bottle into the water. My heart stopped. Who saw me? I tried to look nonchalantly on all four sides. The guys working on their boat in the distance were pre-occupied. Nobody was walking the deck on either side of me—but the two-story condos behind me, with the screened in lanais could be a problem. I counted on everybody's less than perfect eyesight over the age of fifty.

I looked over the railing, where a minute ago, I was searching for a manatee. Now I provided a lethal object if one of these sea creatures surfaced and swallowed it. I considered lying prone on the deck, reaching into the water, but my arms weren't long enough. Maybe I could go back to the condo and get a pair of barbecue tongs.

By the time I got back and explained my solution to Paul, he said, "Don't be ridiculous. By now the current has carried it out to sea—to some unfortunate dolphin."

The Lawn or the Garden—
(a no-brainer to me)

Paul loves his lawn—God only knows why. He says it's good exercise to mow the lawn, even though he's at the gym or the golf course almost every day. After mowing, he often comes into the house, stressed about the latest weed that's plotting to destroy our lawn. But in no time at all, he's back out there—the spreader filled with weed killer, fertilizer, and seed.

"Why don't we just get a lawn service?" I asked.

"For the same reason we don't get a gardener. You like working in your garden. I like working on my lawn."

He is finally resigned to the occasional yellow spots from the grand-dogs' pee. I googled to get a solution. "Paul, just fill up a bucket of water, and dump it on the spot to dilute the dog urine right after they go." Of course, that didn't happen.

His latest complaint is that our Delaware back yard grassy area is shrinking, as the trees are getting bigger, with the limbs blocking the sun. Oh, and here's the big one. My hydrangeas are also getting bigger, and they block one of the sprinkler heads for the lawn irrigation. "I can't get my grass to grow, and it's starting to look like a parking lot," he laments.

"Well, that's an easy fix. Just move the sprinkler head."

"I am not rearranging the sprinkler heads to accommodate a hydrangea!"

"Ok—how about this," I said. "We rip up the lawn and plant ground-cover, like ivy or pachysandra in its place? Or, I could expand my garden. I saw on the Internet that tidy green lawns which are always thirsty and need pesticides are starting to be replaced with lovely perennial gardens. They're friendly to the environment and ensure the survival of the bees."

That apparently didn't even deserve a response, as I heard him revving up the lawn mower in the driveway.

Parental Mistake?

You try and do your best, but sometimes, despite all the agonizing, you still screw it up. Brian was graduating from high school and planned to take a summer job in Block Island, a lovely New England vacation spot. We could see it in the distance from the Rhode Island beaches where our family rented a cottage for many years. He was going with a friend, and they were planning to get a job shucking oysters.

At the last minute, his friend found out that he couldn't join him. So—what to do? Brian convinced us he was now an adult. He would be ok and was looking forward to the adventure.

Paul was working, so I drove Brian up from our home in New Jersey. We took the Block Island ferry over to the island and walked a few yards to the restaurant, where the kitchen manager directed us to the housing in the back. I helped Brian carry his stuff up a very narrow stairway to his bedroom. His roommate, who looked like Attila the Hun, was sitting on the edge of his bed, staring at us.

The knot in my stomach formed as we walked out of the building and into the bank to open a checking account. We then found the Catholic Church, went inside and said a prayer.

I left on the next ferry, the knot in my stomach now a tangled mess. As the ferry pulled away and we waved to each other, his body became smaller and smaller. I hung over the rail, bawling my eyes out. What have we done?

The minute I got off the ferry over in Rhode Island, I immediately ran to the nearest pay phone (this was 1994), and called Paul at work. Still crying, I said, "We made a terrible mistake!"

"If he's not happy, we'll go and get him. I'm sure he'll be fine. It'll be a growing experience."

When Brian was back on New Jersey soil in less than two months, I asked him what he did the day I left on the ferry. He said he was

feeling a little lost, so he decided to go see a movie. The only one playing was *Schindler's List*. Way to go, Brian. I bet that movie put you in
a lighter frame of mind.

I can't imagine leaving anyone, anywhere today without a cell
phone in my hands and theirs. Those days were the real test of our
trust in Divine Providence.

Yep—She's My Daughter

"You'll never guess what I did!" Annie said to me.

"That's usually my line," I replied.

"Well, in New Jersey, you can't pump your own gas. When the attendant returned my credit card, I thought he was done, and I drove away—with the nozzle still stuck in my car!"

"What?"

"I know—it was awful. I heard a noise, and as I looked in the rear view mirror, I saw the attendant throwing his arms into the air." Boy, I guess this genetic stuff is really true.

"And then what?" I asked.

"I got out of the car to find that I was dragging the hose behind me. I felt terrible and asked the attendant what I should do, but he was hysterical." He kept saying, "How am I going to tell my boss?"

"Annie, this is like a scene from Seinfeld. I can picture George Costanza saying that."

"Do you think I should have given him money?"

"I wouldn't worry—they probably have insurance for these things. You did the right thing by asking him what you could do and returning the hose. And I'm sorry, but I can't stop laughing."

Persevering Paul

I never met anyone as persevering as Paul. The leaf blower stopped blowing leaves one autumn day and an hour later, there were tools all over the newspaper-covered kitchen table along with parts and pieces of the blower. And when I say this man has tools, Home Depot would drool for some of his. Hours go by. He likes a challenge, until he doesn't. It's never easy for him to admit defeat, but eventually the disassembled leaf blower got thrown into the trash.

He's very patient when assembling things. Like the time he went to bed at 4 a.m. on Christmas Eve (well it was Christmas morning by then), after putting together the miniature kitchen set for the kids. No less than seventy screws and bolts connected plywood panels to plastic. My bleary eyed husband stumbled into bed, proud of his construction skills; and I made sure I let all of our holiday company know how hard Santa Claus worked on this project.

We recently bought a new computer chair for me to use while writing at my PC, one that spins on its axis with a cushy leather seat. He asked the salesman if it was difficult to assemble, and the answer was, "No, it's a piece of cake—even comes with its own screwdriver."

"Paul, it's only a $20 fee to have it assembled here"—went to deaf ears. After hoisting the huge, clumsy box into the car, we drove home and he lugged the huge, clumsy box into the house. When he dumped the plastic bag of all different size screws onto the rug, along with three pages of diagrams, I knew that what lie ahead would not be pretty.

The next hour was spent swearing and sweating, while attempting to insert screws into holes that didn't line up. I prayed he wouldn't have a heart attack over this stupid chair. I wanted to strangle the sales clerk. Every ten minutes, I was alternately dismissed into the kitchen or called back to balance the seatback as he neared the finish line. Over a glass of wine that night, Paul admitted he should have let the store assemble it. The whole thing was exhausting. I was proud of myself for never saying, "I told you so"—out loud.

The Buzz Bus

Our adult kids like to occasionally include us with their friends and activities. Some we politely decline, as it's past our bedtime, but the celebration of our oldest daughter's fiftieth birthday wasn't one of those times. It was all a big secret to Sharon.

We surprised her by driving from Delaware the night before, spending her birthday at the nail salon—topped off with the buzz bus that evening. "I don't understand what this is," I said to her husband. "Oh, you'll like it. A bus is taking us to all the places we went to while we were dating, including past her sorority house at URI."

"Oh, how sweet! And then we come home?"

"Well, no. We stop at our old hangouts for a drink."

"We've got to have a back-up plan," I whispered to Paul. We left a car in the parking lot of a restaurant that was in the middle of this bar-hopping bus trip, so we could bail out without being noticed.

After getting on the bus, everywhere I looked, I was face to face with grade school photos of Sharon, blown up to life size images. Then I noticed a few of the guys loading spirits onto the bus, along with chips and birthday cake. "OK," I said to myself. "Don't embarrass your daughter on her birthday." I used to get car sick when I was little. I outgrew it, but I couldn't chance the combination of motion, alcohol, and cake.

I sipped on one drink the whole ride. I think I had a good time, based on the video someone took of me singing along to "Sweet Caroline," while hanging on a pole for balance on the moving bus. We bailed out early, according to plan.

"What time did you get in last night?" I asked them all the next day.

"Probably an hour after you did. I guess we're catching up to you in age."

"You'll never catch up."

One Example of Our Family Text Thread

On a trip to Eleanor's home in New Jersey, on one of our marathon visits to the kids, she posted a picture of Paul onto our family text thread—standing with his belt anchoring an ice pack to his back.

Eleanor: Lord help us.

Annie: What is that?

Eleanor: Ice pack.

Brian: Ice? Hey guys, they can't be driving all over the east coast. This is what happens.

Annie: Aww, what happened to his back?

Eleanor: Hurt it making scrambled eggs for breakfast. Don't ask me how.

Sharon: Lord help us.

Coffee Isn't What It Used to Be

"Let's go to Starbucks, Grandma." I was so touched that a grandchild who just finished her first year of college wanted to hang out with me.

It had been a while since I treated myself to Starbucks. Years ago, during my Christmas shopping break at the mall, a caramel latte was my special treat.

Anyway, I've been out of the loop. My granddaughter asked me, "So—what do you want?"

"A coffee, I guess. What are you getting?" I asked, while trying to remember the Starbucks name for small and large.

"I'm getting a venti iced matcha tea with oat milk and two pumps of vanilla syrup."

"Okay—not sure what you said, but I'll get the same." I figured I was doing the barista a favor, by not having to remember another smorgasbord of words. Although, actually, the real reason was I would have needed another 15 minutes to figure out the coffee menu. I could have gotten plain coffee, but not this adventurous grandma.

She handed me a clear plastic cup with—pureed asparagus? No, it was that iced matcha thing, and it was actually pretty good. I tried to fool my brain, by telling it they added heavy cream instead of oat milk.

Their family usually has half-and-half for my coffee when we visit, but they forgot the last time. "Don't worry. I can use whatever you have." So the next morning I poured watery oat milk into my coffee and, well…

The Washing Machine

We don't see our kids as often as I'd like, as the closest family lives two hours away. So when we go, I transform into the Brady Bunch's Alice. It makes me happy. And I just sleep in the car on the way home. Paul doesn't like the way I drive, in case you're feeling sorry for him.

One of the families in New Jersey had the washing machine going non-stop. Clothes and towels—lots and lots of towels. For a minute I thought I was doing laundry at the Hampton Inn. I thought I broke the machine on the last day we were there. I put a last load of Paul's and my clothes into the washer, and turned it on. The lights on the digital dashboard didn't seem to advance from the sensing cycle. Paul was anxious to get on the road, so I stared at the little green light over the word "sensing" as if staring at it would make it move to the wash cycle.

I thought of everyone's advice with everything digital. I unplugged the machine, plugged it back in, and did it all over again. I googled do-it-yourself fixes on my iPhone, and started poking buttons, getting the digital panel on the washer all confused.

With my elbows on the washing machine, I lifted my face to heaven and prayed, "Please!" Next thing I knew, the machine gave a little jolt, and advanced to the wash cycle. For all I know, there was never anything wrong. The next time—I am leaving the room after I hit start.

When I told our daughter I thought I broke the machine, she laughed and said, "I've gotta tell Bill," our son-in-law in Rhode Island. Bill swears he ends up buying a big-ticket item every time we visit them. First it was the dryer. Now, to be clear, that had nothing to do with me. I got there to babysit their toddler when Mommy was going to the hospital for baby #2. I went to switch the wash, only to find a dryer full of wet clothes. My laid back son-in-law said, "Oh, we can deal with it later."

"No we can't!" I said. "We're going to have a ton of newborn baby laundry in a couple days—plus everybody else's!" Dryer repaired.

Next year their furnace went. I was manning the house when the repairman came and agreed with everything he said about how unsafe it would be to just do a repair. So a new furnace was bought.

The next visit, the garbage disposal broke. I told him it wasn't me. Their kids seem to think the disposal will chew up avocado pits.

The last thing that broke (this time it *was* because of me) was a wine glass—the only one left from a set that Bill's deceased mother had left to him.

We still get invited to their house.

Calamity Jane

Sometimes I feel like Calamity Jane, you know—a clutsy person always getting into accidents. However, I thought that to be accurate in my writing, I should research Calamity Jane. It turns out that she was actually a raucous free spirit who lived in the late 1800s.

Anyway, why can't I ever get injured doing something heroic, that could make the local six o'clock news? No, I'm just an older woman who got wacked by an elevator door because she thought she could make it through the tiny space. I didn't think I broke a rib or anything, but I must have done something to cause the pain.

When it didn't get much better, Paul and I drove to an ortho practice and saw a spine doctor. By the way, the last few doctors I researched looked nothing like their pictures on the Internet. Their dark brown hair turned magically gray. Add pandemic face covering, and it gets a bit suspicious.

The x-ray showed no break—yes! But wait, he started checking my reflexes. I almost kicked him in the face when he tapped my knee with the reflex hammer. I took my socks off (so glad I had a pedicure), and he rubbed the handle end of the little hammer along the sole of my foot. I couldn't remember from nursing school what the normal reflex response was other than laughing. Then he had me walk with one foot in front of the other, like they do in sobriety tests. He looked serious. "I'm ordering an MRI to make sure there is no disc damage."

I told my sister and she laughed, saying, "You never could walk with one foot in front of the other!"

It turned out that all was well. I have a new respect for elevator doors.

Please, Officer!

"Come quick—look out the window!" Paul calls to me. "A red fox is walking through our yard."

By the time I got to the window, it retreated into the trees.

It reminded me of the time we were visiting Sharon's family in Rhode Island years ago. I was steering the car into their driveway at dusk and saw a fox run under their side porch. The hairs stood up on my head, as I thought of our little grandchildren. So—I called the police.

"Officer, I just spotted a fox going under our daughter's side porch!"

"And?"

"Sir, aren't these dangerous? They have very small children."

"Ma'am, they are indigenous to our area. They pretty much mind their own business, as long as you don't provoke them. In fact they are probably more afraid of you."

And then there was the day a long time ago—I was driving on the Fourth of July when a cute little bunny ran under my car. I heard a crunch and as I looked through my rear view mirror, saw his furry little body quivering.

"Oh my God—I killed a bunny!" Not knowing what to do, I drove around the block (back to the crime scene), half hoping the little thing hopped happily back into the woods; but there it was, barely moving. So I drove home and called the police.

"Officer, I just ran over a bunny on Foothill Road."

"And?"

"Well, I was hoping one of your officers could check it out."

"Ma'am, you do know it's the Fourth of July, and all my crews are out on the highways. I'll get someone to look into this if they can."

I could just imagine him rolling his eyes and putting out an APB to his officers responding to real crises, providing them some comic relief. "Bunny on Foothill Road—probably dead."

Amtrak Newbies

Our adult kids: "You two have got to start taking the train. We don't like the fact that you're driving up and down the east coast at your age." Paul and I looked at each other. Damn—when did we turn ninety-nine?

"We really ought to give it a try," I said to Paul one day. "I mean, if we can maneuver the airports with their long, winding security lines and spend hours flying through the stratosphere above the clouds, I am sure that Amtrak will be an easy adventure. I can't believe we've been married fifty years, and never took the train."

I think the reason we tend to drive while visiting out of state is because we are terrible packers. You've heard the expression, "When in doubt, throw it out." Well, we have our own system when we pack. "Where to begin? Throw everything in."

We planned our maiden voyage and booked the Amtrak from Wilmington, Delaware to Kingston, Rhode Island. We walked into the large lobby of one of America's oldest train stations, and looked in awe around us. We were immediately swept into the arms of one of Amtrak's designated grandpas—a Red Cap agent.

"And where are you going, sir?" asked this sweet elderly man, decked out in a red blazer and a red cap. After showing him our tickets, he said, "Ah—headed to New England. Well, that would be on Track 2, up the escalator." As he noticed us nervously eyeing all our paraphernalia—"Don't worry, I will help you with your bags."

Ten minutes before our train's arrival, just as promised, there was our Red Cap, grabbing luggage, all the while corralling a few other deer in headlights and up we went on the escalator.

At each of the multiple stops along the way, the conductor scanned the phones of new passengers for the reservation barcode. I was really impressed how he kept track of passengers leaving, boarding, and walking up and down the aisles to the café car and lavatory.

He reminded me of the photographic memories of young wait staff in restaurants. Without writing anything down, they approach a table of ten and commit everyone's order to memory. "Medium rare— oh, you just want a little pink? Well ma'am, that would be medium. Anchovies left off your Caesar salad?"

"Just add my husband's anchovies to my salad," I pipe in. And on she goes to eight more diners.

Anyway, I'm digressing. The ride was uneventful, as we got an appreciation of ponds and small towns that were always hidden from view when driving.

The only twinge of panic I got was when, at the first stop, the voice coming over the overhead speaker announced that passengers could depart from the train only at door #3 and #6. Oh geez, is that the door to our car? After making a trip to the dining car for a snack, I realized that maneuvering through a moving train was not for the faint of heart. How the heck was I going to find the right door in time, dragging my luggage before the closing doors sliced me in half. A wonderful, soft spoken conductor came to the rescue again.

"Don't worry, ma'am. You get off at Kingston, and all doors open up there." I figured Kingston, home of the University of Rhode Island, required adequate egress for the crowds of out of state students schlepping back and forth to school.

"We made it!" I said to Sharon, who came to pick us up.

"How was your trip? No big deal, right?"

"Yep, no big deal." I winked at Paul.

Hiatus from Writing

Once I started seriously writing about funny things after retirement, I didn't think I would ever stop because, well—it was fun. But then we decided to move—again. Let me back up a bit. We raised our children in New Jersey and then lived in Virginia's Shenandoah Valley for eleven years. Our next move was to our retirement home in Delaware in 2012, and we expected to stay there. Near the end of our ten years as Delawareans, we had a few neighbors who moved closer to their children. And then—*our* children started with the recurring comment, "You're getting older and you need to be close to at least one of your kids."

One day I said to Paul, "I guess it's really not fair to expect our daughter to drive two hours if we're ever hospitalized or in rehab for any length of time." And so we started to look. We rented various Rhode Island summer cottages for a couple weeks each summer since the kids were toddlers, and as our oldest lives minutes from these beaches, it seemed like the obvious choice. Although I told our Rhode Island family, "Be careful what you wish for."

We found nothing we could afford for over a year, and decided that since we had a nice home in Delaware, we'd give up the search. And then, in the summer of 2022, while renting our summer cottage, a teeny tiny house (not much bigger than the cottage), appeared out of nowhere.

Well, any house with two full bathrooms isn't exactly *teeny* tiny, but it is tiny. The first visit to the house with the realtor gave me the usual knot I get in my stomach when spending a lot of money or making a big decision. The house was cute, but...

A couple of our kids came along on our second visit, Facetiming their siblings. "Oh Mom, this is the perfect place for you and Dad!"

"It is?"

"Yes—it's adorable!"

I started to see the house through a different lens. My new rose colored glasses saw a cozy dollhouse—with no stairs, hardwood floors, the sun streaming through lots of windows, and a perennial garden. What more could I ask for!

And on that day, my writing went on a hiatus. Truth be told, it actually went on a hiatus a couple months before the saga of the house, as I decided I needed to do more marketing, besides social media, for my first two books. But that's the story for another chapter.

Buying a new home is not for the weak, in body or mind. To my older friends—do these transactions when you can still hold your eyes open long enough to read the voluminous material that needs to be signed. Since most of it is now on the computer, have a grandchild on call for tech support. It was hard to stay ahead of the back and forth communication. Every time we'd hit *send*, a new e-mail came flying through.

Selling Our Delaware Home and Getting Rid of Stuff—Again

We traveled back to Delaware to put our house on the market and figure out which of our belongings would fit into a house half the size of our current one.

"Selling our home should be a piece of cake, compared to what we went through to buy one," I said to Paul. Wrong. There were still lots of forms to sign; and we had to deal with a home inspector who took his license very seriously, checking our home with a fine toothed comb for anything that could cause havoc for the new residents. We paid big bucks for a structural engineer to examine something we never even noticed in the basement, which he determined was not a safety issue.

I was thrilled to start throwing things. I went on overdrive with *my* stuff, because I knew there wasn't much chance of Paul parting with some of the tools he never uses, the boat stuff he never uses, and a lot of other stuff that doesn't fit into either of those two categories.

I no longer had to paint our dark wooden piece of furniture an antique blue, which I procrastinated doing for years—because it was getting donated. Oh—and the artificial seven foot pre-lit Christmas tree. Paul had a hard time with that; but it was an easy one for me. "Paul, it's too big for our new home. Plus, two of the limbs are reinforced with twine because they sag. And last year we had to add a string of lights to replace the duds."

"Ok, ok. Just one more thing we'll have to spend money on—in addition to the tiny house that costs twice as much as what we paid for our Delaware home that's twice the size."

I sent tons of iPhone pics to our kids with images of wall decorations and knickknacks that were hibernating in the basement. "Anybody want this stuff? No infighting please—first come, first serve."

"No thank you," came back from all four of them. This happened even with the china given to us for a wedding present. You see, when we moved to Delaware, I decided to temporarily store the china in the basement, unpacking essentials first. Well, it never left the basement in ten years. We just got used to a very casual, minimalist life style.

Apparently, our children felt the same way, so I figured I would sell it to a china retailer, and divide up the proceeds between the families to help with the grandkids' college expenses. Their Great Grandparents, where the china originated, would like that. When I checked the china resale website, I found that each piece had to be wrapped carefully and shipped 500 miles away. And—they were only interested in a few odd pieces of the set, which happened to be cracked. Contrary to thinking my Havilland Limoges was going to bring in enough money to finance a grandchild's Harvard education, I was very disappointed.

I then went on Facebook marketplace, for the first time, and included a picture. I was expecting my phone to ring off the hook. Nothing—not even *clicks* of curiosity.

I don't know why I should struggle with my Catholic guilt, getting rid of Grandma's china. After all, Jesus was a humble person, and I am sure china was not high on his list.

Anyway, I came to a compromise, and it was pretty ingenious, I thought. I wrapped ten sets of cups and saucers in newspaper, and packed one for each grandchild, to give them when they had homes of their own, as a keepsake. The rest I donated.

The mental energy I spent on *stuff*! And yes, I know that some stuff is full of memories, but I already have precious memories of my maternal grandparents in my head— sitting around their big oaken dining room table, watching my grandfather carve the roast beef, the wonderful trips to the zoo, the apple tree that shaded their backyard, and the way my Grandma used to call my Grandpa "Edward."

As a child, I visited them over Christmas vacation one year. One of my Christmas presents was a tiny sample of lipstick to use when playing dress up. They brought me to their friends' home after I

62

slathered on this red lipstick, and never made me wipe it off. They were so tolerant of me, the oldest of their thirty grandchildren.

When visiting them one summer (I was about nine), I wanted to make believe I had a hair salon. So I dragged a twin mattress into the bathroom, laid it over the edge of the tub and the toilet seat top, and had my five year old sister lie on top, proceeding to wash her hair under the faucet. After drying her hair with a towel, I found a bottle of (hand?) cream and spread globs into her wet locks.

Ok—enough about memories and moving on to the closing of our Delaware home. All that was left was the walk through. The new owners brought their realtor with them, and as we chatted with the buyers (a lovely couple), the realtor was as neurotically efficient as the home inspector. I could hear toilets flushing, water faucets turned on and off, and the hum of the microwave. Good heavens—let's move on! We signed the papers and the labor pains were over. Off we were to greet our new baby in Rhode Island, which had its interior freshly painted in our absence.

Wakefield, Rhode Island

Moving day went smoothly. Our kids came to help, and rather than haphazardly ripping open boxes, I asked them to do what they were good at, and let me deal with the boxes at my own pace, one by one. So while Paul dealt with the TV service people and garbage collection, etc., the kids cleared out the October debris from the gardens, and hung all the artwork and photos in strategic places on the walls. They accomplished what would take us weeks to do. And in no time the tiny house was turned into our home—our final home. I told Paul he'll have to pull me, kicking and screaming, out of this one.

Wakefield is a village within the town of South Kingstown, Rhode Island. The Atlantic Ocean, minutes away, skirts its south shore. Wakefield is small and after vacationing here for years, you'd think I knew it like the back of my hand. No—I needed to use my GPS to find the hair salon a month after I got here. Really sad, considering it takes less than ten minutes to get from one side of Wakefield to the other.

One good thing is that the hospital is down at the end of our street. Can't miss that. In fact, the kids said that if Paul has an emergency, they'll just sit him in the wheelbarrow and roll him down into the ER. Good thing he has a sense of humor.

The Murphy Bed

We were going to use our pullout sofa from our old home for overnight guests in our second bedroom, which would also serve as my writing room with a desk top computer. The room is small, though, and I pictured couch cushions strewn all over the floor when the bed was pulled out.

Our kids said, "You need a Murphy bed. They have some really nice ones that would fit the style of your room." Hmm—my vision of a Murphy bed was a cartoon image of a bed snapping into the wall, the sleeping person unaware and helpless—trapped forever. Google enlightened me with gorgeous Murphy beds that looked like wall armoires—some with bookshelves to the side. I was overwhelmed with all the choices which, by the way, were pricey.

Then I found a site with the pros and cons of Murphy beds. Yes, at last. I love looking at pros and cons. The first con was that they were a bit clumsy and awkward to pull off the wall and lift back up—for the elderly. Ha—I don't think we are elderly, although I am happy to take on that description for discounts. But, here was a no brainer safety reason. Case closed.

A week before moving day, our Rhode Island daughter (and soon to be our new neighbor), sent a text informing us that their neighbors were getting rid of their Murphy bed, and would give it away—free, to us. All we needed to buy was the mattress. I hate revisiting a decision I already spent too much time on the first go around.

I told Sharon, "We already told the movers to transport the pullout sofa. How about we decide when we get there and have a look at it. We need to test it and see if it's elder friendly." The photo won me over—tall and sleek, made of pecan wood.

We had the movers put the pullout sofa into the garage. The weekend after we moved in, Paul checked out the Murphy bed and said it wasn't that difficult to maneuver. So seven guys who weren't quite sure what they were doing, disassembled it from the wall, with a few minor injuries. They transported huge pieces of wood over to our house in a pickup truck and stacked them in the garage. A week later a handyman who *did* know what he was doing, installed it onto the wall. While even I can pull it down, it's really a two person job to raise it back up.

I absolutely love our Murphy bed. In fact, that's where I slept when Paul got COVID. I could talk softly on the phone, as I didn't disturb him on the other side of the house. I brought snacks to bed, watched TV, and pretended I was single. I knew it was a matter of time before I would get COVID too, but I dreaded seeing the pink line show up on my test strip (and it did). This meant there was no reason to continue sleeping in the Murphy bed. And since Paul proof reads my book, I want him to know I really was delighted to move back into our bedroom.

The only issue with the Murphy bed is that when it's opened up, space in the room is tight. I did another face plant when I tripped over the leg of the bed while our kids were here for the holidays. I didn't lose a tooth this time, but had an embarrassing bloody lip through New Year's. I can't afford to fall on my face again. With lipstick, my puffy lips are starting to make me look like a seventy-four-year-old with too much Botox, and without lipstick—Mike Tyson.

Space

We never lived this close to any of our children. I used to envy those whose grandchildren could run around the block after school to Grandma's house for cookies and milk. Well, it finally happened to us, a little late, as the youngest of the Rhode Island grand-kids is in high school.

I wondered before the move what it would be like, giving up the space I usually had surrounding me. My eyes bulged when Sharon said to me, a week before we came, "Boy, I can't wait to whip you into shape, Mom." (I guess she doesn't consider walking through the supermarket and Marshalls—exercise.)

"Sharon, I hope you don't think you're going to show up at our doorstep at 8 a.m. to go for a power walk with me. Daddy and I don't roll that way. We're still in our bathrobes at nine."

"No Mom, when you're up and about, I'll come over with our little dog and we can take a walk now and then." I heard her telling a friend, weeks later, about our conversation, down to the exact words I said. Did I hurt her feelings?

These were just growing pains, feeling each other out. We actually like their spontaneous visits, and wish it could have been like this for the other kids.

In truth, we are very lucky. Our families always gathered in the summer at rented cottages in our favorite state, and now that we live here full time, there's less pressure to make all the visits coincide.

I was concerned about intruding on their space, too. Soon after we moved in, and after going to their home for dinner a few times, I got a call on a Sunday afternoon. "Mom, why don't you and Daddy come for dinner. I have chicken cooking in the crock-pot."

"Sharon, I don't know. Sunday is family day."

"Oh, for heaven's sake. You are family."

When Paul was discussing the football games with her husband on the phone later that afternoon, I took the phone and told Bill about my conversation with Sharon. "I really think your immediate family needs alone time together on the weekend."

"Stop overthinking it. Just come."

So we went and ate Sharon's crock pot chicken.

Writing—I Love Marketing—I Hate

The marketing of my books has something to be desired. I've done readings and book signings, and I tried to create a platform on Facebook. Although it didn't help when I wrote happy birthday to a deceased Facebook friend whose profile was still up. It also didn't help when I replied to a complimentary comment on one of my posts with a mad emoji.

There's a learning curve with everything. At my first book signing, while sitting at my table of books, I tried to grab everyone coming into the bookstore. Ah—there's a twenty-something. "My book would make a great Mother's Day gift for your Mom."

"She died last year," he responded.

During COVID, the book signings had to be outside. It was August in a beach town—not very smart of me. I'd have made more money with a lemonade stand. Lots of sweaty bodies looked right past me as they hastened to the cool ocean water.

So I got the idea of making cold calls to over a hundred independent bookstores throughout the country, getting the phone numbers and the genre they preferred from a great computer data base. You might remember that a saleswoman I am not. Selling Girl Scout cookies and the grade school magazine drives soured me to sales. But on the other hand, I am a phone talker, and carry on conversations with not just my friends, but also the Verizon agent in India or the Amazon customer service agent. So the cold calls didn't intimidate me as much as I thought they would.

I had many rejections, more than I care to count, but others asked me to send them my website. I received a fair number of store owners who offered to give me a chance and put my books on their shelves. But the process was tortuously slow. Some required more than one call back and numerous follow-up emails.

I have to keep telling myself, "Books don't sell themselves." Well—the exception being the famous person who holds her book up in front of the Today show audience. So, Savannah and Hoda, if you are reading this, I can be ready at a moment's notice.

I'm back in the saddle and working on book number three. Writing keeps me happy and sane. Marketing—absolutely not.

New Doctors in Rhode Island

It seems like every time I get comfortable with my doctors, we move—and the search begins anew. It was so much easier when I worked in hospitals. While family practice physicians don't usually see patients in the hospital, the specialists do. From observing them and their patient outcomes, I could hand pick whoever seemed like a good fit. Here in Rhode Island, I use the recommendations of family, new friends, and Google.

I research them for their education and experience. My sister always makes sure they went to a prestigious medical school. "How do you know they didn't finish at the bottom of their class?" is always my question. If they followed their residency up with a fellowship, I'm very impressed. Internet searches also have patient reviews, which of course I get sucked into reading.

I know you can't judge a book by its cover, but one time I had to do a double take when the physician walked into the room. The intelligent looking, dashing guy in the picture with wavy, dark hair aged twenty years! Not a deal breaker, though. Age brings wisdom, hopefully. You know—they say women are vain. The female physicians actually had more honest portrayals in their online photos.

I did take a chance once and chose a physician with excellent credentials at the opposite end of the age spectrum. He looked like a junior in high school in his online photo—and in person.

The initial visit to acquaint myself with my new primary went well. A nurse practitioner asked me questions regarding my medical history. Every time she thought I was wrapping it up and she was finished typing, I would say, "Oh, here's another thing."

I always prided myself on being so healthy. But this long list of ailments really lengthened, since I related my history to a primary ten years ago, after our last interstate move. Well, it's now on file, so I won't have to recite it again, as my next move will be to a cemetery.

Buying the Area Rug

We were trying to find an area rug to partially cover the hardwood floor where we placed our forest green sofa and floral chair from Delaware. The carpet from our old home was too big for the great room in our tiny house. While I'm aware you can mix prints and florals, I also know that you have to follow some simple rules. I studied up on Google sites so as not to make any rookie mistakes. No matchy-matchy combinations or the opposite—a nauseous mix of geometric shapes and colors.

"We need to get moving on the area rug purchase, Mary Ann. Let's go down to that flooring place in town today." I froze.

"Honey, we need to take our time. Our floral chair is creating a challenge. Green and red are not the popular colors now. I have been looking online, and blue and gray are all over the carpet sites. Also, the pattern can't be too busy because it will make the room smaller than it is."

I could tell I was losing him. The same way I get lost when he's watching CNBC, the financial channel, where all the commentators scream rapid fire while charts and graphs fly over the screen.

But back to the area rugs. "Paul, you may not realize it but I am constantly checking online. Also, every time I go to the supermarket, I stop in Marshall's next door, and flip through their area rugs hanging from the ceiling. I'll know the winner when I see it."

A month later, on a Saturday afternoon Paul said, again, "How about we go to that flooring place in town?" I couldn't put him off any longer, so fifteen minutes later, we were flipping through samples and rug remnants, as the salesperson popped by frequently to see if we needed help. Paul was ready to close a deal with a credit card more than once.

"Honey, just have patience," I said to a glum looking husband as we left the store. A few days later, Marshall's came through. "Paul, can you drop everything and come over to Marshalls? I think I found a carpet I love!" He was there in five minutes, glad that the carpet episode was over. I think he would have agreed to a jungle animal design—anything, just to end my annoying search for perfection.

The Apple Support Person

I have great admiration for computer programmers who actually enjoy looking at screens with all their symbols and numbers for hours on end. We had a 12-year-old granddaughter who went to summer camp to learn coding. I didn't want to admit I hadn't the slightest idea of what coding was, so I consulted Google on my iPhone. The next day an advertisement popped up on my phone with opportunities to learn how to code. Good grief—that Big Brother of mine again. No, thank you.

I like what technology gives me when I want to get lab or x-ray results off my patient portal, or directions on my GPS. It's the *input* of information that makes me cry. Like the time I tried to make a website. Nothing I clicked made sense, and my eyes started to well up. Now, you know that techies love this stuff. So that's when I picked up the phone.

One day I messed up my iPhone and couldn't *send* mail. I figured I should at least see if Google had the answer. No luck. After an hour of clicking on sites, on multiple days, I called my sister Betsy to calm me down. She asked, "Did you call Apple?"

"I called someone, but I don't remember who."

"You probably called your wireless service provider."

Next thing I knew, she had me and an Apple support person in Canada on a three way conference call. This nice man with a deep voice popped a red cursor on the settings of my phone, directing me where to go and click. Within seconds, I could now send mail.

"If you were not thousands of miles away in Canada, I'd give you a hug and take you out to dinner!"

After we ended the conference call, my sister texted, "I'm not thousands of miles away and I have a restaurant in mind."

There's nothing like expertise when you need it. I confess there were times in my married life, when our four kids were little, that I fantasized being married to a pediatrician. And in later years, to a Geek Squad member from Best Buy; although—realistically speaking, an eight year old kid could solve my tech problems—and I'd get to keep my current husband.

Talking Through Walls

"I can't hear you through the walls," I've heard numerous times from Paul. I love it when I can get back at him and say the same thing.

"Did you just text Dad?" asked Annie, our youngest, on one of her visits.

"Yes, why?"

"He's in the same house—two rooms away!"

"Honey, it's easier than screaming to a deaf person, and I don't feel like walking to the kitchen for a simple question."

When I got no response from Paul I yelled, "What's wrong, Paul? You didn't get my text?"

"Mom, this is pathetic." Our kids sometimes compare us to Seinfeld's parents. That's because they were too young to watch Archie and Edith.

On our family text thread, with all the kids participating, I sometimes kill two birds with one stone. In the middle of planning for a summer vacation, I texted, "Paul, since you're in the kitchen, can you turn the oven on to 375?"

"Aren't they in the same house?" popped in Eleanor.

Still Mulling Over a Hip Replacement

Apparently, it's not just a matter of what the MRI shows. The patient has some say. "If the pain and stiffness affect your quality of life," the new Rhode Island ortho doctor told me, it may be time.

I would have been more comfortable if he said my leg was about to fall off if I didn't get an immediate hip replacement—or, "You're fine. A little PT will fix you." I don't like gray areas. I danced at the last wedding we attended. And I can climb up on a step stool to put things on the top shelf of our walk-in closet. Does that count as a good quality of life?

"Yes, but you can't get up off the floor without pushing off the coffee table; and you nearly yank the railings off the walls going upstairs," said my husband.

I saw a Facebook video that night of a ninety-year-old woman in leotards doing an olympic gymnastic routine on the parallel bars. She's either got good genes or it was photoshopped. Those damn genes. Thank you, Mom and Dad.

"How about I start physical therapy again?" I asked the doctor. "We moved and I've been lax with my home exercises."

"Sounds good to me. We'll meet again in a month. If you decide in the meantime to go for the hip replacement, call the scheduler in my office."

So I started PT. The therapists said multiple times that my joints and muscles were tight. That's not a good thing? Apparently not, but I guess they must have seen potential. In fact, I felt like I was training for the gymnastics World Cup—lunges and stretches and—here's a good one. They put an elastic band over both calves while I was standing. Then I had to walk sideways. I felt like hot stuff that I could do this. I brought the printout home with the photo of a very buff guy doing this exercise. His leg spread against the resistance band was at least two feet. Guess I have a way to go with that one. Six inches won't make World Cup.

Timing Is Everything

I have decided that most guys have awful timing and no working filters of speech. Here's an example. Paul decides to try and kill a fly in the middle of an important conversation, smacking a dish towel down on the arm of his recliner and saying, "Missed again."

"This f'n fly has been eluding us for three days, and you have to try and kill it now?"

Then there's the topic of finances. Well, there's no good time for that conversation, but first thing in the morning before I've had my coffee and he's already watched an hour of CNBC is definitely not the right time.

I'm usually jumping all over Paul when he's about to call our married kids at dinner time. "Paul—they have lives. This is the worst time to call." And there's his faulty filter, when talking to our kids: "Your mother doesn't want me to say this, but..."

To be fair, I don't always have the best timing either. "What were you thinking?" asked our daughter, who stopped in one evening. The banging of pipes and some choice words emanated from the bathroom.

"You asked Dad to fix the shower head at eight o'clock at night?"

And the other day when I called our daughter, Sharon, on a weekend at 8 a.m. She picked up the phone on the first ring and in a groggy voice, asked, "Who died?"

"Nobody," I said and hung up. Hopefully, she thought she was dreaming.

Mom Jeans

I buy jeans infrequently, because it's so painful, (as you may remember from my first book). And I usually do research to see what's in style. Not that it matters. You couldn't pay me to buy the low-rise. Mid-rise can also be a problem. If the waist isn't high enough, you end up with a roll that wasn't there before you put on the jeans. And if the fabric of your blouse is the slightest bit clingy, you're taking a chance.

A couple years ago, I went into a store looking for *mom* jeans, the new high-waisted jeans that cover the end result of babies, bagels, and brownies. Even the young kids are grabbing them up. The store apparently was not informed of this new trend, and I couldn't find them anywhere. I asked a sales woman who looked about my age, and she didn't know why the store didn't stock them; but she told me my best bet were the Lee *flex fit* mid-rise jeans, which she was wearing. She said they ride higher than normal mid-rise and proceeded to whip up the bottom of her sweatshirt so I could get a visual. Boy, that's salesmanship. I bought the jeans and, by darn—she was right.

Driving Lesson

I don't remember much about teaching our kids to drive, although I do remember one of their teachers gave lessons for a fee. Babysitting my kids' kids is really teenage sitting with some chauffer duties—until they get their driver's permit.

"Wanna go with me so I can practice my driving, Grandma?"

They all make fun of my driving, but I guess they don't care if I am in the passenger seat—anything that gives them more time in front of the steering wheel.

"Are we going to a parking lot?" I asked.

"No, but there's a neighborhood a few blocks away that is never busy and I can practice my parallel parking." So we got into the car.

I went into teacher mode. "Now, what is the first thing we do before we start driving?"

"Check for passing cars."

"Well, yes, but before that."

"Put your seatbelt on."

"Okay, and?"

She was stumped, so I added, "Check your gas tank?"

"Oh right!"

She glanced at the dashboard and I hear, "How much gas do I have if the arrow is a couple millimeters above E?"

"Enough to coast down the hill to the gas station."

I think I confused her, giving her tips while she attempted to parallel park. "Actually, Grandma, my dad told me to do it this way."

"Oh by all means, do it his way!"

She was getting discouraged. The motor started making a funny sound.

"What's that noise?" I asked.

"Don't worry, Grandma. It does that all the time. It's going to the garage this week."

"Are you bringing this car to your test? They might fail you before you even get a chance to drive, if they hear that whining sound."

She passed the test a week later.

Déjà vu

My decision-making skills are always challenged in a shoe store, which goes back to childhood. I wonder what Freud would say about that.

If I wear my current sneakers any longer, my toes will look like those of the ninety-year-old patients from my hospital days. I started researching sneakers with wider toe boxes, as gravity has shortened my torso but spread the toes of my feet. Sorry for the visual.

My daughter, an avid walker, was wearing a brand I never heard of as yet. You need to get these, Mom. Funny—how when you have something on your radar, like a sneaker brand, you start seeing them everywhere. I started looking at the feet of walkers passing me by, the feet of the physical therapists, and at the feet of restaurant wait staff. Wow, this new brand had hit the ground running.

I finally ventured into a shoe store that specialized in sneakers. As I walked in, I realized this was not the outlet kind of store I was used to shopping at, where I could be anonymous as I pulled shoes off the stacks, rarely asking for help. No, this was more like the old fashioned shoe store with excellent service. It brought back memories of my mother asking me if my Buster Brown shoes that the sales person put on my feet felt comfortable. For some odd reason, I could never give a straight answer, driving my mother and the sales person nuts.

Now, in the sneaker store, I was eight years old again, trying to act like I was seventy-four and confident. The patient sales lady brought out a few pairs of sneakers, and I was sure this new brand everyone was talking about was going to be a perfect solution for my aging feet. Maybe my expectations were too high. They sure didn't feel as if I was walking on a cloud, like my daughter and the online reviews said. But maybe I just needed to break them in. I was proud that I finally pulled the trigger and picked a pair, not the perfect pair, but a pair none the less. If this was a final sale, I would have brought them home and that would have been the end of it.

Instead, the saleslady said I could bring them back if I wasn't satisfied, as long as they were not worn outside. That's the kiss of death for me.

I tried them on at home, and immediately realized they felt too clunky—not good for a klutzy person who already trips over her own feet. I walked around the house, trying to like them. Then I started reading online reviews. Well, I wasn't the only one to find something to not like with this popular sneaker! Although, to be fair, not one sneaker brand had 100 percent five star ratings.

I dreaded bringing them back the next day. I know it's their job, to make the customer happy, but all I could think of was the pile of shoes and boxes she had to put away the day before. And what if I can't find a pair I like the second time around.

To make matters worse, the salesperson and I got into a conversation of how we just moved to Rhode Island. It turned out, she lived up the road from me. Oh great—if I return these and go to one of those sneaker outlets, or maybe Amazon (where you can really be anonymous), she'll see me on my walks sporting brand new sneakers—not from her store. My mother was right. Never do business with friends or relatives.

I went back to the store the next day. Like a big girl, I opened the door, and with a smiling face, explained the situation. She brought a pair of two different brands, and after trying them on, I said, "You won't believe this, but they both feel great. I really can't decide, so I will get both. I deserve them, right?"

She rung them up and after ripping open the boxes at home I tried them both on. "OK," I asked myself, "how could two pairs of sneakers that felt fine in the store manage to feel different at home?" If you're getting a headache reading this, imagine the knot I had in my stomach and how ridiculous I felt. Why couldn't I make a better decision before I spent money on two pricey pairs of sneakers?

I jumped into the car before I would lose my nerve and returned one of them. Then I told the saleslady that I was keeping the other with the intent of breaking them in.

I also told her she probably needed a glass of wine after me. I got home and immediately put them on, went outside and scuffed the soles in the gravel from the street—now I have to keep them.

How I Learned Instacart

Our oldest grandchild left for her freshman year at a South Carolina college and came down with COVID a week later. The unfortunate students were cohorted in a nice dorm meant for visitors, with private showers and microwaves. Her meals for the day were dropped off outside her door. After the doorbell rang, she looked through the peep hole and when the delivery person left, opened the door and picked up the bag of food. It could have been a history lesson on what it felt like to have the plague or leprosy in medieval days. I mean, minus the microwave and shower.

Feeling her mother's angst, I offered to send a goodie bag in a box to the COVID dorm. I was in the supermarket, throwing microwavable oatmeal and soup into my cart, when my cell phone rang. It was Sharon, her mom, telling me she called the health office for the address, and was told that everything goes first to the college's main campus postal service. She added, "By the time it is rerouted to her, she might have sprung the place. The only things that will go to the COVID dorm directly are delivery services like Instacart, Door Dash, and Grub Hub."

"Ok, no problem," I said to her, thinking about how I've never used these things. But, how hard could it be, so back onto the supermarket shelves went my stash of nourishment.

I found Instacart on the computer, and felt like Alice in Wonderland, falling into a hole of all kinds of delicious food, soups, and medicine. All that was needed was a credit card. What cave have I been hiding in?

The computer directions to order were surprisingly easy—I guess made for other grandmothers who had a strong need to send chicken soup to their sick grandkids.

Another time, I thought I'd surprise Sharon on her birthday. Paul and I were under the weather, so since we couldn't go out, I decided to have Instacart deliver a birthday cake and sushi to her door when she got home from work.

That evening, her husband said, "We live two blocks away! Why didn't you call me to pick it up? You just spent a delivery fee on top of the bill."

"Maybe because I wanted to imagine her delight when answering the door?" Some things are worth the extra money.

The Supercenter Alarm

"Attention loyal customers—please leave the building immediately!" came over the intercom, loud and clear. In case anybody didn't take this seriously, the intercom directive blasted through the store again. Holy crap, what is going on? Flashes of TV newscasts flashed before me. As I left my shopping cart behind, I flew out the door. Funny—I wasn't worried for my life. I was just hoping I'd find my half-full cart if I ever got back into the store. A few minutes later, as we all stood in the parking lot, another announcement came that the alarm system *test* was over. Now why didn't they alert us that this was about to happen, so heart defibrillators wouldn't go into overdrive? We were vacationing in Florida at the time, and it made good conversation that evening.

The only other time I was whisked out of a building was also in Florida. I went to a walk- in clinic for a problem. I was dressed and waiting to be discharged from my visit when the fire alarm went off, and I could tell by the look on the faces of the personnel that this was the real thing. It turned out to be a small fire at the nail salon next door in the strip mall. While I waited for clearance that all was ok, I sat on a bench, outside the back door, chatting with the doctor who treated me, and noticed the lady on the adjoining bench wearing a hospital gown. "I just had an EKG," she said. I would love to see the rhythm strip as they yanked the leads from her chest.

Next time I go out, I need to look presentable, which I wasn't that day. You never know who they are going to interview on the six o'clock news.

My Brain

Cobwebs, after a summer rain, are mesmerizing, with sparkly rain-drops scattered throughout the web's geometric maze. Cobwebs in my brain are not so beautiful—or helpful. And I know why I get them. It's called overthinking. Facebook has all kinds of memes and posts about that, and peaceful solutions to get your perspective back. So, social media is definitely good for some things.

Speaking of Facebook, somehow they caught on that I started reading posts similar to, "Ten Outfits Mature Women Should Never Wear." I started getting targeted posts like, "Twenty Keepsake Treasures Your Children Don't Want," and "The Thirty Worst Cities to Retire In." Going down these rabbit holes is fodder for the overthinker.

As I crawled into bed that night, I thought I'd better check and see if we just moved to one of the worst retirement places. No wonder I get insomnia. This year I am going to scroll past these posts. I will henceforth be on a need to know basis. That is, until I have insomnia and reach for my phone to find, "Ten Ways to Beat Insomnia."

1 Put down your electronics.

My Favorite Spectator Sports When It Comes to the Grandchildren

If someone asked me what my favorite sport was when watching the grandchildren, I would say, "Well, it depends."

"Depends on what? Your favorite grandchild?"

"Of course not! It depends on the weather and the sport itself." I always liked baseball and basketball. For one thing, I have a greater understanding of both. I sat in our living room and watched the Phillies with my Dad on our black and white TV, back in the 50s. Richie Ashburn and Robin Roberts were my heroes.

When we had our own family, I loved the tension when Brian, our son, was at bat. Nothing beats the crack of the bat, sending your child's ball into home run territory.

Years later, I get to see our grandson, Joey, whack the ball, while sitting in pleasant seventy-five degree weather. Though to be accurate, the temperature did climb at times to steamy heights. And—I was not allowed to petition the umpires to call the game when the temperature climbed above ninety even though it was *my* grandchild trapped in his padded catcher's gear.

I have my own personal history for my interest in basketball. I played on our elementary school's team, knowing I would make the all-stars in high school. Except, once I got to high school, I lasted only two years on the team, getting barely a wrinkle in my mustard colored, skirted uniform.

Our daughters, sadly, didn't do much better in high school, getting into the game for the last forty-five seconds of play.

But the granddaughters—wow. And how nice to remember the lingo of basketball. "Nice layup! Great bounce pass!" and—"You're wrong on that foul! She charged right into Ella."

And did I mention the temperature controlled gym?—where volleyball is also played, and which I knew nothing about until I became a grandma.

Gymnastics is also a sport I know little about, but I had to get up to speed since a granddaughter was bringing home medals. I couldn't even do a cartwheel when I was little. Nope—just summersaults. Although I pronounced them tummersaults until a friend informed me I was saying it wrong.

With soccer and lacrosse, weather can be a deal breaker to Paul and me being spectators, especially if the wind is whipping. I don't get how they can expect these kids with spindly legs to play on a frigid November day when I need two blankets to keep warm. And again, I'm not allowed to appeal to the refs to call the game. We got stadium seats for Christmas with foam cushions to keep our bottoms from freezing on the metal bleachers. I think we're expected to give equal time to the cold weather sports.

The biggest problem watching soccer and lacrosse from high up in the bleachers is my sight. The fact that I'm still learning the ins and outs of soccer, lacrosse, and ice hockey (I forgot that one), along with my failing eyes—I've had to devise a way to keep track of our grandchildren. I try to keep my eyes plastered on their uniform jersey's big number. It works, most of the time—although once I was waving and calling to the wrong kid for half the game.

Any sports I left out? Ah, horseback riding. I watched so many episodes of Netflix's Heartland, that I admire one of our granddaughters who can get these large but gentle beasts to follow her commands.

And then, of course, there is one activity that weather and comfort are non-issues. Thank God we have a granddaughter who has picked a theater instead of a stadium in which to perform. So I live vicariously through Abby. Belting out a song from *Annie* is as exciting to me as a goal or home run!

Don't Ask Me to Drive If You Have a Tender Post-op Belly

Boy, you really feel old when your daughter needs a hysterectomy. Unfortunately, she wasn't a candidate for a laparoscopic procedure and needed an abdominal approach, which required a larger incision, and she was in surgery for almost three hours. I won't give you any gory details.

I was happy to spend a week with her, cooking, folding laundry, and bonding. I got to take her to her first post-op doctor's appointment one week later. It was a twenty minute drive, and we were on the road only ten minutes when she said, as she cradled her belly, "Mom, it hurts when you keep hitting the brakes."

"Oh, I'm so sorry, honey." I had flashbacks of when it was my turn to drive her team to basketball practice years ago, as the nausea started to overtake them.

"Mom, you know the speed limit on this highway is fifty miles per hour, right? You are going thirty."

"Oh, you're right. I was just thinking about when you kids were little."

I accelerated to fifty, lowering my head so I could see the odometer, which was hiding below the steering wheel. "Mom, every time you lower your head, you drop back down to thirty. Why don't you just drive, and I'll let you if you're keeping the speed."

I started to giggle, a nervous giggle, which made her do the same. "Mom, my belly hurts! Please stop laughing!" But neither of us could stop—that is, until her giggles turned to crying with real tears. Oh my God, what have I done to her?

She offered to let me go in with her for the post-op visit, which went well, learning that she was on target with her recovery.

Before we left, her surgeon asked her if she had any more questions.

"Well," she asked," looking tentatively at me, "Is there any chance I could drive home? My mother is a wonderful nurse—but a terrible driver."

"Are you able to turn and look over your shoulder, without pain?" the doctor asked, and hearing the affirmative, gave her permission. Was I offended? Now really, how could I be? She did well on the smooth ride home, and I was glad I could take part in her building some post-op confidence in her driving ability.

I Learned How to Be an Adventurous Cook from Our Kids and Grandkids

I don't have a sweet tooth, so I don't like to bake. But *cooking* on the stove—not measuring and just going by the taste, is my kind of joy in the kitchen. The older I get, the more adventurous I am. The credit for that goes to our offspring, who like to experiment. I love their enthusiasm for cooking.

While I was visiting one of the families recently I was throwing out expired spices and salad dressings, etc. I hadn't visited for a stretch, because of Covid, and their cabinets, bulging with expired condiments, were calling me. While I was having a blast going through the shelves, I came across some enticing stuff: citrus chili paste, lemon grass, buttery cashew salad dressing. Also, they are very big on kale. I like it if it's mixed with other vegetables, or in a soup. We had dinner there one time when Paul picked out the kale, like a five-year-old. Guess who ate his kale?

Paul is a good sport with my cooking. He grew up on fairly bland food, so when he asks, "What's for dinner tonight?" I'll say, "It's a surprise." I learned my lesson the week after we got home from our honeymoon. When I told him what I was planning for dinner, he said, "I don't eat that." That's the last time he ever said that, because he wasn't involved in the choice anymore. Don't feel sorry for him. He really likes my cooking—too much, according to the scale.

I found that I can't go wrong when I throw some broccoli (charred in the oven) into a pot with whatever else I find in the refrigerator. And if you haven't cooked broccoli this way, trust me that the blackened broccoli florets are not burned—they're charred, with a wonderfully different taste.

I always have to hold back a smile, when I have an older friend for dinner who is not up on the latest food trends. As they take a scoop of the charred broccoli I get a furtive glance that says, "Oh the poor dear. I'll pretend I didn't notice she burned the broccoli."

The ingredients that can make or break a dish are the spices and herbs. Salt and pepper reign supreme. I could live on pasta with a tad of olive oil, salt, and pepper.

The fun comes when you get adventurous with cajun spices, soy sauce, turmeric, and a host of others. I used to be afraid of hot pepper flakes, but noticed that the chefs on the TV cooking shows often throw a sprinkle into their dishes. Go crazy with the spices and if you panic at the end, melt some mozarella on top.

Two caveats:

I love my butter, but I try to use extra virgin olive oil, instead. (I really do.)

I NEVER use cilantro—ugh!

Messes

I don't like messes. Well, I need to clarify that. I make huge messes in the kitchen when I cook. My mother's sewing machine was in the kitchen of the home where I grew up, with patterns and fabric spread all over the kitchen table. How she would have loved her own sewing room.

In the bright, sunlit rooms of our daughter's art studio (in addition to her hanging artwork), there are easels, paints, brushes, canvases, frames, and mixed media material all over her work space.

I am a writer, which creates a mess in a small circumference around my computer. For sure, my brain works better with less around me.

Back in the days of my hospital nursing career, the messy scene in the aftermath of a Code Blue, with the code cart and IV poles thrust into places where the bedside table and chairs once stood, was always unsettling to me.

I know, you thought this was a humor book, but I'm almost done.

I don't like thriller movies that involve destruction of Hollywood sets, and those reality TV shows depicting the sad mental health condition of hoarding.

But to me, the two most distressing scenes are the real news videos showing earthquakes and other natural disasters alternating with the devastation of bombed out cities; resulting in the worst mess of all—broken bodies and minds.

Oh dear, that topic really escalated—enough depressing thoughts. I have a hopeful slant on this later on.

My Plant Identifier App

Remember the 1964 Jewel Akens song, "The Birds and the Bees?" A song about a "thing called love" had lots of hungry hearts fantasizing about their future one and only. It seems like only yesterday.

Now, "the birds and the bees and the flowers and the trees" have curious seventy-year-olds identifying them with apps on our iPhones that our grandkids showed us how to use. We can now identify birds by their chirps and warbles, just by tapping a button when they start singing.

I can also identify the flowers in my new Rhode Island garden, just by snapping a picture. And did you know that not all wild flowers that look like Queen Anne's Lace are in fact Queen Anne's Lace? No—there is a poisonous wildflower that looks like its twin, aptly named, poison hemlock. The reason I was looking on my plant identifier is that there is a lot of this unnamed wildflower in our garden. I couldn't have the SPCA come after me for annihilating our grand-dogs—plus the guilt, and the gnashing of teeth. Nope, this had to get resolved quickly.

I didn't need to worry—the plant identifier on my phone told me it's not poison hemlock. But it's not Queen Anne's Lace either. It's called "ground elder." Kind of a weird name—so I'm telling everyone these wild flowers are Queen Anne's Lace, a much prettier name befitting my pretty garden.

My New Vacuum Cleaner

It's pretty sad when the highlight of your day is a new vacuum cleaner. The old canister (its hose taped together with duct tape), got banished to the garage in our new home. And when we finally made a decision on an area rug to cover our hardwood floors, I had to move beyond my beloved Swiffer cloths. I wanted a cordless, but oh—the choices! Not just brands, but different versions of each brand. I pored over the reviews and asked for opinions from my Facebook friends.

The online review that won me over was the guy who said if I was doing all of the research that he did, in addition to surveying friends—I should stop right there. He found one that was next to perfect. And, it happened to be the same one that was in the running for me. So I clicked *Buy*, before I could change my mind.

Paul was looking over my shoulder to see what all the commotion was about, as I yelled *hallelujah* when I chose my dirt sucker. "A little pricey for a vacuum cleaner, isn't it?" he asked.

"Honey, this vacuum will outlive both of us. You get what you pay for."

I feel like it's still a toy, and I keep looking over my shoulder for the absent cord. As for my dear Swiffer cloths, "I won't throw you aside, like an old boyfriend. I'll use you to dust the furniture. You will always be my first love."

The Decision

Two things made me decide to say yes to a new hip. I really do want to walk more, especially now that we live in Rhode Island. Such pretty gardens to see with all the gorgeous hydrangeas that love the salt air up here. Plus, on the practical side, my dearest husband isn't getting any younger either, and if he has a medical issue in the future, I don't want to be recovering from hip surgery at the same time.

Anyway, the date is set.

The hardest part was the decision. Of course, nothing ever goes smoothly. A few weeks before my surgery date, I tripped and wacked my knee. So besides going back and forth to physical therapy to strengthen my hip muscles in preparation for surgery, I now needed ice on the knee of my other lower extremity.

I started watching hip replacement surgeries online—really fascinating. Then there were some YouTube videos with handsome ortho docs who gave helpful advice for before and after surgery. One of them said that there were three things we needed to remember in the recovery phase, and the first was, "Don't fall!" While the surgical procedure videos did not keep me up at night, the advice did. I picked up the prescribed post-op walker the very next morning to practice.

What are all these boxes showing up at our front door?" asked Paul.

"For when I get my hip done."

"You planning to have a party the day you come home?"

"No, these boxes are filled with assistive devices—a long shoe horn, some contraption to get my socks on, and a claw-like picker-upper. Oh, and a three inch high square of foam so it's easier to get out of a chair when I'm recovering."

"I thought those were all my jobs?" He looked a little disappointed.

"Aww—you can certainly help me, but I have to learn to be independent. Oh by the way, the sneakers didn't come yet."

"You already have sneakers."

"No, these are slip-ons. All the support, but you don't have to tie them."

The Big Day

The time had come.

The house was in perfect shape. The nesting instincts I had fifty years ago when our children were born came right back, just like riding a bike. Since I couldn't fit even one extra roll of toilet paper in our tiny house, I had the garage decked out with non-perishables resembling a tornado shelter. "Mom, you know that Dad can go to the grocery store when you get back from the hospital."

"I know. But I'll sleep better if I know we won't run out of paper towels and toilet paper."

I planned to come home the same day but, as advised, I packed a bag—just in case. We showed up to the hospital at 7:30 a.m., and my adrenalin started to pump, though not out of fear. Just like when I had my hysterectomy twenty years ago, I was looking forward to seeing things from the other side. I guess only a nurse would get this, but I had sent and received patients from the OR and I wanted to be more than just an observer, as if I was watching an episode of ER. I wanted to experience being the recipient of the rhythm and intensity of the OR.

I was to have a spinal, followed by IV medication to keep me in la la land during the surgery. After I had my IV inserted in the pre-op area, the anesthesiologist came in to meet me.

"Where do you administer the spinal?" I asked.

"Here in the pre-op area," he responded. And with that I sat on the edge of the bed, as one of the nurses told me she was giving me an IV sedative. I was all hyped up to feel the spinal begin its magic, and I would be wheeled into the OR suite with the bright lights as everyone was scurrying around. Maybe I'd even catch a glimpse of the shiny hardware about to take the place of my ball and socket hip joint.

But no. I missed it all—that is, not in a wakeful state. The nurse in the pre-op area was barely finished instilling the IV medication, when I found I was waking up in the recovery room, now called the PACU (post anesthesia care unit).

And I can't say I was the least bit comfortable, as I opened my eyes; but the angel of the PACU had me pain free in minutes. Plus, I remembered from my pre-op talk with the surgeon, that there was a local anesthetic injected into my hip joint, before ending the procedure, and it would last over 24 hours.

I don't know what I was thinking, planning to go home the same day. It was an option, if the physical therapist thought I could be discharged safely, but thank God I didn't pass the safety test. And they weren't taking any chances with me, after reading my *fall* history in the chart.

Speaking of safety, never fear that you will be at risk for sloppiness in today's hospital procedures. I gave my name and birthdate to a hundred staff members during my short stay. Even the nutrition staff asked me, to make sure I didn't get someone else's green beans.

I walked around the room the same day with my walker and a physical therapist, learning the dos and don'ts to protect my new hip; and the next morning I learned how to put on pants and shoes. I was discharged after my last hurdle, going up and down two steps with crutches. I had a tough time going down, and realized at that point the terrible shape I must have been in before the surgery. The therapist said, "Don't worry. The physical therapist who will come to your home will work on this."

"Be honest," I said to the therapist. "What percentage of competency would you say I am in comparison to other post-op hip patients?" He hesitated—hmm, that wasn't good.

"I would say about where fifty percent of patients are the day after surgery." Would it have killed him to say fifty-one?

Recovery

I find it incomprehensible that I was *not* in excruciating pain, during those first couple weeks post-op, considering a piece of metal was shoved down my femur. And good thing, because movement was the path to recovery, alternating with rest periods. Yay—I could look at my iPhone without guilt. I made a ton of calls to current friends, old friends, and any acquaintance who was willing to answer their phone.

Our home looked like an assisted living facility for a couple months. But was I glad I ordered the *hip kit* from Amazon, with the grabbers and long shoe horn, and the ingenious contraption to put on socks. After a while, I was using the grabber for other stuff besides pulling my sweatpants over my feet. Instead of looking despairingly at the ice cubes that flew to the floor from our hyperactive ice machine, I could pick each one up and fling it into the sink. And I could reach the candy on the high kitchen shelf that I was hiding from Paul.

One day I decided to empty the dishwasher, against Paul's admonitions, while he was at the gym. I bent over slowly to pick up the silverware compartment so I could set it on the counter and empty it. Somehow the plastic side popped open and silverware flew all over the floor. In fact two sharp knives were sitting inches from my bare feet. "How the hell am I going to get these off the floor when I can barely touch my knees?" And then—ahh, the grabber! So I spent the next fifteen minutes picking up one piece at a time.

I got a brief glimpse of what it was like to be physically challenged—the big difference being that I knew this was temporary. I was walking by myself, using my walker, towards the elevator after a post-op doctor's appointment. As I was about to press the button, I dropped my glasses to the floor, where the frame cracked and the lens popped out. They were cheap reader glasses from Walmart, but the dilemma was how I was going to pick them up off the floor, without my *grabber* tool. Just as I was about to backtrack into the doctor's office to ask the receptionist for help, the elevator door opened and a sweet little lady with a working spine solved my problem.

My post-op instructions said that I should avoid comparing my recovery to others. Good thing I read that, as I definitely was not my surgeon's poster child. In fact, I was sure that other patients were doing ballet moves at this point. If only I could tie my shoelaces and maneuver my toenail clippers. I figured it was time to schedule a pedicure.

The walker which I used when I first came home from the hospital brought back flashbacks of my mother, when she visited. Paul and I would be sitting in our chairs drinking our morning coffee when we'd hear the rolling wheels of my ninety-year-old mother's walker rumbling over our hardwood floor into the kitchen.

Paul really stepped up to the plate. In fact, he's gotten more fastidious than me when he loads the dishwasher or vacuums with our new Dyson cordless. A tiny potato chip hiding under a counter doesn't have a chance with Paul and the Dyson.

When I graduated to a cane, I noticed the wide berth that people gave me in the store and church. It was kind of fun, while it lasted, as I'd poke it into the air while making a point to Paul.

Physical Therapy—Again

I love my physical therapists. Not only are they encyclopedias of knowledge regarding muscles and joints, they seemed to know the answers to all my post-op worries every time I felt a pinch, or a pull, or soreness. They were physical therapists and psychotherapists all in one. "Oh, you're doing great. You lifted your leg two millimeters higher since last week!"

Their patience with all of us slow movers fascinated me—patience that I don't have. I'd have to hold back the urge to poke a needle into my client's derriere to get them to move faster. But no, these physical therapists not only have knowledge and patience, but they have vision, and they know how to pull their clients to their potential.

A little segway—Paul injured his shoulder at the gym. So he was in PT too. One day we were there at the same time. I was pulling on a band to stretch my core, face to face with him, doing the same. Staring into his eyes, I said, "How romantic! And this is what married life has come to."

It currently looks like we have a home gym, with all kinds of weights and rubber stretchy things that we are supposed to be using for our home exercises.

Our daughter, and new neighbor, stopped at our house on a Saturday morning on her way home from the gym. "It's 10:30! You're both still in your pajamas!"

"It's not what you think," blurted Paul.

"And by the way, what the heck is going on in here?" she asked, as she eyed us pulling on the rubber cords.

"Impressed, huh?"

"I guess you two plan to be around a few more years."

"Well, yes. But for now we just want to be limber enough that we don't have to call you over to tie our shoes."

Nothing Is Easy

At least once a month, either my social media gets hacked, or I lose my debit card, or I need to get medical records from our last location—I could go on.

And nothing is easy, when it comes to this stuff. I've noticed that computer programmers are not minimalists. Some of the screens look like hieroglyphics. I usually end up working off two computers. On my iPhone, I ask Google how to fix something on my desk top, and then begin pulling up multiple screens, thinking I must be blind because I can't find what Google tells me is there.

I would much rather hear a voice on the other end of a phone line. But that's not easy either. "Press 1, press 2, press 3, press 4." I start to daydream, and have to call the main number all over again—all this just to get a voicemail after I finally hit the right extension. Some places play hardball. None of the phone options match what I need, so I think they want me to end the call in frustration; but oh no—I'm a fighter. I start yelling "AGENT!"

The world's communication has gotten more complicated and cluttered. Even though most businesses would rather deal with communicating online, there are others that send envelopes stuffed with voluminous amounts of paper—did no one learn the art of being concise?

And oh—the trees that met their demise in my recycling bin! I never asked for the piles of weekly coupons and sales, so I don't feel a twinge of guilt.

I'm Turning into My Mother

It happened to my mother. She was already petite, but was very tiny by the day she died. Well, I have lost almost an inch since sixth grade, when I was 5ft 5 in—the second tallest girl in my class of fifty-five kids. I hated being so tall.

My vertebrae are slowly collapsing, but I now can fit into petite clothes, which expands my choices. That's about the only advantage. I sadly need a stool to climb into bed. I did draw the line at attempting to get things off the top shelf of our kitchen cabinets. When we moved, I got rid of top shelf kinds of stuff—you know, the kind of platters and pitchers you will never use unless you are planning a banquet for the United Nations.

I don't mind being the smallest in a group picture of our grandchildren. Although, each time the camera comes out, "Grandma, I can't see you. Come up to the front row."

Speaking of my mother, as she got older, she was still very independent. When she visited us, her bedtime routine took forever. And it began at 7 p.m. Prematurely, I am turning into my mother at bedtime.

I usually take my shower at night, and to be honest, I have a lot of preparation for bed: fill the Keurig water chamber for our morning coffee, brush and floss, take my medications, put my early morning dose of thyroid medicine on my bedside table, charge my iPhone, use my hand lotion, and dab a little Vaseline on my lips to soften my scars from past falls. I'm sure I forgot something.

I like to start early, like my mother. Otherwise, if I wait till Paul is in bed trying to sleep, I have to tip-toe around the room, like a burglar, using my iPhone flashlight to open drawers, etc.

My mother used to drink a cup of hot milk before bed. That—I don't do.

Low Profile Box Spring

Remember the story about my buyer's remorse after our purchase of the extra firm mattress that cost a fortune a few years ago? Well, either I got used to it, or the mattress got used to me. What I never got used to was the height, and since I am apparently shrinking each year, we decided to switch out our box-spring for a low profile model. (You can skip this amazing tidbit of knowledge if you own a platform bed.)

So, if you never heard of a low profile box spring, I can educate you, as I did my usual research. Most box springs are nine inches high. Low profile box springs are about five inches. Now, I know that losing four inches of height doesn't sound like much, but it meant that I could throw away my stool. Now I can actually get into bed like a normal person, instead of a jack rabbit.

This was a public service announcement for ladies with shrinking spines.

A Different Kind of Floater?

Weird things come with age. "I think I have some floaters in my eye," I said to Paul, as we were sitting in the waiting room of the orthopedic surgeon.

"What are floaters?"

"When you get older you can see little specks or squiggly lines that float around the inside of your eyeball. They're usually not harmful," I said as I pushed stray strands of hair away from my eyes, which of course did nothing. Then I tried to blink them away.

"If they're inside your eye, I don't see how blinking is going to help."

"You're right." I started to panic. "I don't remember these kinds of floaters before. I can't even concentrate. In fact, they're not floating—they're flittering all around the inside of my eyeball!"

I turned to face Paul and started to ask "Do you see anything?" But before I got the words out of my mouth, he reached over and grabbed something that he squashed on his pants before I could find out what it was.

Oh my God—a bug? It must have been stuck in the mascara of my eyelashes! I bought this new brand of mascara that has finally made me look like I have my own eyelashes. It really sticks to my lashes and obviously really stuck to that bug, or spider, or... Eww! I guess I'll never know. Rambo took care of that.

The Lawn and Garden in Our New Digs

Remember the book, *Men Are from Mars, Women Are from Venus*? Well, that explains our relationship quite well. Here is an example. As you know, Paul loves his lawn. Our Rhode Island home has less green grass than our Delaware home, but he throws the same amount of energy into creating the perfect lawn. The grass has dutifully slurped up fertilizer and weed killer. The bare spots were liberally sprinkled with all species of seed meant for sunny or shaded areas by Johnny Appleseed.

While I appreciate his efforts—I, on the other hand, have lower expectations for our lawn. Green is good enough. Dandelions are pretty.

Paul has low expectations for our gardens. "Paul, we need lots of color." It was killing me to not be able to crawl around the gardens of our new home, because of my recent hip replacement. The previous owners left a lot of perennials, so we wouldn't start from scratch, but I wanted to make it my own. I turned into the Master Gardner anyway, delegating jobs to Paul.

"What do you mean, I have to move a bush?" he asked, as if I directed him to burn the house down.

"Some of these boring bushes have outgrown their space. When I get the go ahead from the doctor, I'm driving to the plant nurseries and getting some fun, colorful flowers for you to plant."

"You know, we don't have to go crazy," he said, seeing dollar signs and hard labor in front of him.

After spending our kids' inheritance on clematis, hydrangeas, and daisies, we both got to work. I felt like the foreman on a building site, giving him directions on where to place my new little babies, pointing with my cane.

For being such a good sport, I got him a little present online (no, not a golf club). It's a tricky little contraption, called "Grandpa's Weeder." You can dig out your dandelions without bending over. He loves it.

109

Netflix or Sports?

We compromise when it comes to evening TV viewing. I like sports when it's the playoffs. Period. I don't focus well during their season games. In the playoffs I pick a team, usually the underdog, unless it has a personal history for me—like Phillies baseball. They evoke memories of sitting next to my father watching the Phillies on our nine inch black and white TV.

Most other times, we compromise. We watch an hour of Netflix, and then Paul switches to sports. Don't ask me how, but I got him to watch "Call the Midwife," a TV show based on the memoir of a midwife who worked in the 50s delivering babies in a poor section of east London. I think Paul liked it because of its overall artistic excellence and historical facts, with a hefty dash of humor spliced throughout.

You ask, "Wasn't he queasy seeing approximately two births a show?" The answer is no. It was very tastefully done—never do you see any pelvic anatomy belonging to the "stage mother." The spell-binding part was the arrival of a *real* baby sliding out from under the drapes, appearing as if it was just born, covered in safe, gooey make-up. There were often scary complications, which lent dramatic tension to the show.

Paul resisted watching at first, saying he couldn't understand the dialogue because of the occasional actors with a strong cockney accent, but after turning the volume up and using subtitles, he was hooked. We were exposed to medicine in the 50s and 60s. Some of the most incredible scenes showed, for example, how everyone smoked—in front of everybody. The doctor would be blowing smoke across the desk in his office from a woman, nine months pregnant. I felt better to learn that the cigarettes used on the show contained only herbs. As times changed, and the medical world learned the perils of smoking, this message was written into the show.

Swimsuits

By early summer, I was able to go to the beach, which was fifteen minutes from our new Rhode Island home. While my legs have scattered roadmaps of varicose veins, I never had them removed because, with a summer tan, they looked a lot less like the Pennsylvania turnpike.

However, I wasn't too crazy about adding the scar from my hip surgery to the mix. "Mom—it's just your battle scar. Show it off!"

"It's ok, honey. Swimsuit companies that are sending me ads on the Internet have my back." Somehow all the clothing stores on social media found out I had a hip replacement. I guess I gave it away by googling the surgical procedure and ordering the walker, etc.

So my fingers tapped away on the keyboard, as I looked for sexy swimwear for a seventy- four-year-old—maybe a tankini with a cute little skirt to cover my scar.

I made the mistake of buying from an online swimsuit company that had twenty-year-old models wearing these sexy tankinis. I was so anxious to get my hands on one of these swimsuits, that I didn't check the reviews of this company I never heard of, which were spitting out these wonder suits to gullible seventy-year-olds.

After I scoffed the Amazon delivery from our doorstep a few days later, I was so disappointed after I tried it on. The top had a weird, big wrinkle in the front. Was the top too big, or did the sewing machine screw up? I decided to order the smaller size.

When it arrived, I heard the stitching rip as I pulled the bottoms on. The smaller top was drastically smaller and the fabric was so flimsy I looked pregnant. Good grief, how could a company get it so wrong?

Did I stop ordering? Of course not. This turned into a mission. I finally found an adorable, flattering suit. It doesn't hide my battle scar, but I don't care.

Alerts and Alarms

Can't we just let things happen? Do we really need to be notified about everything?

Paul has atrial fibrillation, a common heart irregularity in older adults, and often treated with medication. After curling into a fetal position in bed one evening, I heard a chime come from his iPhone watch, unlike the others. "What's that?" I asked Paul, who was just drifting off to dreamland.

"Just my AFib," he muffled through his BiPAP.

"Did you take your medicine tonight?"

"Yes, I just did."

"Well, maybe you should try taking it a little earlier."

Another time, late at night, in the middle of my insomnia, I heard his rhythmic in and out breathing in sync with his BiPAP. But I also heard other beeps and chimes, and had no idea which of Paul's devices they came from. Every night just before midnight, a bar of Brahm's lullaby comes from somewhere. Comforting and freaky at the same time.

He has a smart phone and it feels a need to notify him of a burglary five states away, or remind him to pick up his meds at the pharmacy.

Last night, I heard that different chime again, with a green light emanating from his watch. I wondered if it was his AFib. Geez, and I was almost asleep. But I figured I should check. I slowly reached my hand over, as he has these swinging motions with his arms if startled (and he was never even in combat). I found the pulse in his wrist. It seemed strong. The rhythm—couldn't tell exactly. While debating whether to get up and get my stethoscope, I fell asleep. Sometimes it doesn't pay to marry a nurse.

It's Arthritis—Not Arthuritis

Since I graduated from physical therapy, I am moving along quite nicely, albeit slower than I'd like. I told my therapist I am now seventy-four, and I don't mind a little discomfort. I'm not trying out for the elder Olympics. I just want to be safe—stronger muscles to avoid future faceplants.

And it isn't just my hips. I inherited my father's genes, and have issues with my back, neck, and shoulders, too. It's now called degenerative joint disease. I'm wondering if someone named Arthur changed the name, tired of hearing his named maligned by so many elderly (many of them my former patients) calling this disorder, *arthuritis*, instead of arthritis.

I laugh at the irony that I didn't want steps in our new home, but today I walked to our daughter's home a few blocks away to practice going up and down their steps, which I did in PT. Their little Havanese puppy followed me up, and then followed me down. By the third time, she whined, "Make up your mind, woman!"

Every time I fantasize I am going to be like Simone Biles in six months, I get slapped back to reality. I was waiting for a friend at a breakfast place one morning. A waitress walked by, balancing five plates on her arms, piled with pancakes and omelettes. She was going to the restaurant's upper level, which was roped off; and just as I was about to unhook the rope for her, she lifted a leg and with her lithe body, hopped gracefully over the rope, without losing even a slice of bacon. Holy crap—even in my younger days, I'd never be able to pull that off!

I went for a walk that same afternoon. A lady about my age, whose footsteps I could hear were about to overtake me, asked if she could pass. I was about to tell her I was walking slow because I had a hip replacement a few months ago, but I remembered that funny guy in the Progressive Insurance commercial who would say she doesn't need to know that.

We Have a Pact

My husband and I noticed that our four adult kids have become more vigilant regarding our well-being. And I get the paranoid feeling they're on their cell phones the minute they leave us after a visit for a sibling chat. "Before they determine our competence, Paul, we need to have a pact. Otherwise, we may find ourselves at Sunny Acres prematurely."

Recently, I went to the post office for a book of stamps. "Where are the stamps?" Paul asked.

"What stamps?" I asked.

"The stamps I asked you to buy two days ago."

"Oh right. Funny thing—while I was in the post office, I took one stamp out to mail a card, but I have no recollection of what I did with the book of stamps. I hope I didn't stick it into the mail slot along with the card."

A few days later, as I was emptying the dryer, I called out to Paul, "You'll never guess what I found in the dryer!" I handed him the missing book of stamps, which was now a dried up lump of paper with the faint image of an American flag on top.

Another time, Paul was cleaning up the kitchen after dinner and said "Mary Ann, you forgot to shut off one of the electric burners on the stove."

"I have an excuse. The red element light goes on and off. If I had a gas stove with a constant flame, that wouldn't happen."

"I wouldn't call that an excuse. But don't worry, I won't tell the kids."

When Paul or I leave the house to do errands, we normally come back into the house fifteen seconds later for something we forgot. The other day, as I was sitting here typing, I heard the front door open, right on time, fifteen seconds after Paul left. "What did you forget?" I asked.

"My sunglasses."

Ten seconds later, as the door reopened—"Damn it, I can't find my phone."

"I saw it in the recliner, honey."

Five seconds later—"Now what?"

"Can't start the car without my keys."

"Don't you worry. I won't tell the children."

We have a pact, Paul and I. Although one day when I was really mad at him—"You do know that if you don't knock it off, I've accumulated a ton of blackmail that the kids might find interesting."

"And you know—that can work both ways."

This memory thing is so overrated. When physical therapy came to our home after my hip replacement, she had the nerve to give me one of those memory tests. You know—the one where they give you three words to remember. I kept repeating *ball, blue,* and *market* for the next ten minutes, not hearing anything else she said. When she asked for the three words ten minutes later, I proudly rattled them off. We proceeded to the proper use of a walker, and how to get in and out of bed safely.

Then she pulled a fast one. "Can you tell me the three words I told you twenty-five minutes ago?" Did I recite them back correctly? I'd tell you, but I don't remember.

Lost Manuscript

I sat down at my computer the other day to write. I pulled up my manuscript, only to find blank pages with squiggled images scattered throughout. Oh no—did I not close my document correctly the other day?

I tried to close the screen, when another screen popped up and asked, "Do you want to save?" I don't know why, but this question always panics me, so I hit "Yes." A second later, I realized I saved a blank document with squiggles. I wanted to vomit. "You idiot! Why the hell did you save that?" I screamed at myself.

It was my own fault. I am so bad at backing up my writing. I had been working on book number three, and for the life of me, I couldn't remember the content lost, much less the chapter titles of what went into a black hole in cyber space.

"What's all the commotion in there?" Paul asked, as he walked into a room to face a raving maniac. "Maybe I can help."

"No you can't! I checked Google and I'm clicking all these options."

"Uh, maybe that's your problem. Click, click, click."

"You don't understand. I found something that said, *restore previous version,* so I clicked that and it says there IS no previous version. I saved a blank document!" He sat down in front of the computer, feeling confident, as he's gotten me out of these kinds of messes before.

"See, I knew this was unfixable," I cried, as I paced the floor ten minutes later. "Paul, just go to the beach without me. Our kids are waiting. Maybe I'll call Staples and ask them."

Weird things always cross my mind at times like this—and that was the realization that I never got my shingles vaccine. What's that have to do with my computer? Well, you know that if you had chicken-pox as a child, shingles hibernates in your nerve cells, waiting for your immune system to crap out, especially because of stress. I figured that this would qualify.

"Hello, may I help you?" asked the guy from Staples. After I spilled my sorry tale, he told me to bring in the computer tower. He was pretty sure he could resurrect an old version of my document.

"Do you need the wires?" I asked.

"No, Ma'am—just the tower."

I drove twenty-five minutes to the store, and walked in holding the culprit. It was dead in the store on this scorching hot July day. Rhode Islanders were all at the beach. I was greeted by three sales associates. "You also brought the tower, right?" one of them asked as I stood there with the computer screen in my hands.

Oh no—I brought the wrong thing. I felt so stupid, as I do know the difference between the screen and the tower, but after staring at my computer screen for the last two hours, and pleading for my document to come back, I obviously wasn't thinking straight.

The worst part was having to tell my kids what I did. By this time, because of our Hoyt text thread, all our kids knew mom was starting to lose it over this disaster, and were anxiously waiting to hear if the Staples guy could fix it.

I planned to bring the tower back the next morning, but something miraculous happened. Paul, awake at 6 a.m., was on the computer, and while I have no idea how, he found my missing document.

"You need to back up your documents," he reminded me, for at least the hundredth time.

"You're right. And I need to get my shingles vaccine."

Affirmation and Ego

Raising children and working with co-workers requires effort and constant interaction. Hopefully lots of pleasant interaction, but we have the inevitable altercations. You win some and you lose some. It often takes a lifetime for us to mature and let any negativity from these exchanges roll off our backs, leaving our egos intact.

And then there are the interactions with babies, dogs, and strangers—so different.

Notice how little energy it takes to get a three-month-old baby to smile. "Ah—what a gift I must have! She smiled at me!" And the nice thing about babies—they don't care if I sing off-key or a laugh line goes flat.

The same thing is true about dogs. All they require is kindness and a few treats now and then—such little effort for unfettered love in return.

Not owning our own dog or having babies around these days, I can still get my ego fix for the day when I'm out. If I am craving a smile, even from a stranger at the supermarket, all I have to do is smile at them first. It works every time.

Charley

Speaking of dogs, we were in charge of Charley, our local daughter's Havanese for three nights. She's a cute little black and white puff of non-allergenic fur, and very easy. I know—you're confused. It's Charley, not Charlie, and it's a she. They didn't use my suggestion of Petunia when we voted on names.

Sharon gave us a pee-pad. "Put it on the bathroom floor, and if she has to go during the night, she'll go on that." Afraid I would trip in our little bathroom, Paul left it on the floor right outside our bedroom. In the middle of the night, he went to the bathroom and found three little brown gifts on the ceramic tile.

"Probably because I didn't put the pee pad in the bathroom," he said.

"Aww, the poor thing got confused. She couldn't find her doggy toilet in the bathroom. Let's do what she's used to tonight. I won't trip. I promise."

That night, when Paul ambled to the bathroom, he found not only a yellow circle on the pee pad, but another little puddle two feet away on the floor. Hmm, that was weird.

I heard Paul coaxing her into our bedroom the other night to get into the dog bed. "Come on, Charley. Good dog. Time to go night-night." His voice was sugary sweet—an octave higher than usual. I've got to ask the kids if he ever used that voice with them.

The last night, around 3 a.m., Paul and Charley were up at the same time, so he decided to let her outside—without a leash. She's usually a scaredy-cat, so he figured she'd be afraid of the dark and come right in.

Instead, I was lying in bed, half asleep, and heard, "Charley! Charley, come back here!"

One breathless animal and one breathless human were back in the house momentarily.

"She ran right into the street!" gasped Paul. "Being a block from the hospital, I hoped the rescue squad wasn't going to come flying by."

We delivered her back to Mommy and Daddy the following day in one piece. The next few days we kept thinking we were tripping over a ball of fur.

The Summer Influx

"They're about to descend on us," I said to Paul. And I wasn't talking about the Rhode Island tourists—no, I meant our kids with their families for our annual summer get-together. One of the families would stay with us and the other at Sharon's house, a few blocks away. Brian's family would bop in and out, as they have a beach cottage.

While I love my teeny tiny house, I realized I'd better get to work, getting the garage ready for the kids who would sleep there. I congratulated myself on the foresight in getting the floor painted gray when we moved in, and keeping the pullout sofa from the previous house in there. The garage doubled as Paul's art studio (obviously, no room for a car). Trouble was—a conglomeration of tools, Christmas decorations, cleaning stuff, fishing gear, and gardening supplies were piled willy nilly in one third of the garage.

"I'll straighten it up this week," he promised, the week before their tentative arrival. I *yessed* him, as I planned in my brain what I would do on his next golf day. My idea of straightening up is quite different than his. And it involves throwing out. I rearranged a lot of stuff, but as far as throwing out, I would have to have his consent when it came to *his* stuff. If it was joint ownership, I decided to make executive decisions.

But those damn tools! You know, they say you should never marry, thinking you can change your spouse, because it most likely won't happen. Over ten years ago, I thought I could help him organize his tools. From Home Depot, I got a handsome yellow and black rectangular container on wheels, with inserts to hold nails and screws, etc., and a smaller, portable tool box for the usual handy tools. So now, counting the bright and shiny new ones, we still have six containers full of his precious cache of tools, because he could only part with one.

I suggested that he do an inventory on one rainy day. The Patriots football game trumped that idea. Does he really think he's going to be called to the construction site down town? I won't even let him climb a high ladder to replace the smoke alarms anymore—can't be too careful when you're on blood thinners.

So even if Paul whittled down some of his possessions, I needed a room divider. I searched Amazon, and ordered an inexpensive, coffee colored rattan folding screen. The end result was quite nice, I must say. But two days after the teenagers took up residence, it looked like a college dorm, and we almost saw the demise of my precious room divider. I forgot to warn them that it was lightweight, not very stable, and definitely not teenage proof.

Family Dynamics on Vacation

The members of my family all have Type A personalities, some more intense than the others. So, it works very well being a bit separated on vacation, meeting at the beach and for dinner. It was only four days and nights together, but because of Annie, our event coordinator, we made the most of every second. They were big on exercising their bodies—walking, running, yoga, or working out at the gym in the mornings. It gave me time to drink my coffee and do my morning routine of running around the supermarket, replenishing toilet paper and beach snacks. We all did our thing.

I think every mother on the planet prays for no nasty arguments when her ducklings all get together. I am happy to report we got along swimmingly, all of them keeping their eye rolls to a minimum. Speaking of swimming, they spent a lot of time in the water, during the heat wave that we had. I didn't. Like the lyrics from the Zac Brown song, I sat with "my toes in the water, ass in the sand." As much as I hate high heat and humidity, unless the water is 98 degrees, my delicate body doesn't dive in.

We ate out three of the four nights. We're all foodies and had the best time whether it was a beachy place or a bistro. Paul and I aren't used to this constant activity. One afternoon our kids were making last minute attempts to get a dinner reservation for the whole crowd, while sipping sauvignon blanc at the beach. I could hear Paul say, "This is tourist season. You're never going to get a reservation. Let's just go home and use our grille."

"Paul, we are just tagging along," I reminded him. "They're adults, so let them figure it out." Then the event coordinator piped up, "I found a place with an hour wait. One of us will go ahead, put our names in, and wait at the outdoor Tiki Bar. By the time you all shower, the table will be ready."

"That place is a zoo, when it comes to finding a parking space!" chimed in Paul.

"We'll drive you," piped up one of them.

We did have a traditional cookout one day, at our home, with hamburgers and hot dogs; and I wanted to cook my favorite dishes, since we're hardly ever all together—so I'll tell you what I made, just in case you're curious.

Besides hamburgers and hot dogs, I marinated a flat iron steak. My broccoli-bacon salad made the cut, as well as my pasta salad, which I'm still trying to perfect after fifty years. It's different every time. I used to scavenge ingredients from my refrigerator and cabinets to put into the mix, but I've since gone simple. Most of my family picked out the black olives anyway. Now I use pasta drenched in extra virgin olive oil and a little bit of balsamic vinegar, sauteed grape tomatoes, tiny balls of fresh mozzarella cheese, minced garlic, fresh basil, and scallions. The secret is the simple seasoning. Salt and pepper, for sure. I don't measure. I just taste a million times, and no—I don't use the same spoon. Then I add some crushed red pepper flakes (not afraid of them anymore).

I can't forget the gluten free, vegetarian friendly tofu, rice, and beans for those who get nauseous at the site of animal blood. I fried the heck out of the tofu pieces marinated in soy sauce. You really can't over cook them. The tofu cubes just get crispy—and edible.

I collapsed into bed that night, wondering how restaurants get it all together, multiple times a night while catering to everyone's needs—especially someone like me who has the nerve to say to the waitress at a Mexican restaurant, that I don't want cilantro in my food. Isn't that a staple when it comes to flavoring in Latin American and Caribbean cuisine?

Jersey Boys

Paul wanted to take me to see the musical, *Jersey Boys*, for years, but something always seemed to get in the way. Well, the time finally came—this summer at the Matunuck Theater by the Sea in Rhode Island. Either because it was a matinee, or because of the era that Frankie Valli and the Four Seasons were popular, the average age of the audience was seventy-plus. I was wondering why the show wasn't starting on time, when I heard that a busload of residents from an assisted living facility were working their way into the theater. After all the walkers and wheelchairs were in place, the curtains opened.

I hope music can always be a big part of my life, should I live long enough to reside in one of these homes. While watching *Jersey Boys*, I was transported back to the 60s and couldn't sit still in my seat. The actors playing Frankie Valli and the Four Seasons could have been plucked right from Broadway—they were that good.

When they belted out the 1967 hit, "C'mon Marianne," I felt eighteen again. Back then, I remember thinking it was a long time coming—getting another song named after me. In 1957, ten years earlier, a popular version of a calypso song had Mary Ann "down by the seaside sifting sand."

If anyone is reading this who is involved with the running of assisted living facilities and nursing homes, please think about blasting music in the hallways that transport the residents back to their vibrant youth, instead of easy listening tunes that have them napping all day. "What about agitating the residents?" you ask. Well, let me tell you, I will be one agitated little old lady if I am forced to listen to spa music in my remaining days.

I Ditched the Petunia

I kept my pot of "Million Bells" petunias on our patio dining table alive and flourishing all summer. I trimmed, watered, and fertilized. This flowering plant was like my eleventh grandchild.

September came and I wanted it gone (unlike a grandchild). It was still hotter than hell, and the plant started to get a bit leggy. Plus, a tiny white bug was on the leaves. I had to make a decision. I lost interest in fussing over this annual plant which only had a few weeks left anyway. Do I take it off life support, or nurse it along till the first frost.

"Let's invite my sister over with her husband for dinner this week. It's still nice outside, so we can eat on the patio," said Paul. After eyeing the forlorn petunia plant, the decision was made. That afternoon, I went into the grocery store to buy chicken breasts, and lining the outside wall on the way in were a few hundred potted chrysanthemums, their buds beginning to burst with color, and just the right size for the center of the table. I scrambled to get a cart, and threw in a yellow chrysanthemum, along with some blue asters.

"Why do you have two receipts for the grocery store?" Paul asked when I got home and he happened to be browsing the online banking.

"My cart was full of flowers and I didn't have room for the groceries, so I had to make two trips into the store."

"And why do we need more flowers— it's September!"

"You can blame it on your sister. Remember—they're coming to dinner."

Some Questions You Just Don't Ask

"What did you do today?" one of my daughters asked while I was in a high school gym, watching her youngest in a volleyball game. She caught me by surprise. First of all, I can't remember what I did ten minutes ago. I need preparation for an open-ended question like this. And secondly, when my day starts to float back into my memory, I may need to embellish what I choose to tell her. Unfortunately, I can't report that I sent my third book to the publisher, because I haven't.

No—I told her I googled how often I'm supposed to rinse out the filter on my new cordless vacuum. But first I did my stretches. Oh wait—that was after I sipped my coffee on the back porch and prayed for her soul. Then I rinsed out the filter on the vacuum (it was really filthy). And then... oh yeah, I deadheaded my flowers and drove to the grocery store.

Thank God for the book I'm working on. "Sharon, I barely had time to get to my computer by the end of the afternoon!" Even if I just changed a couple of words in my manuscript, it wasn't lying. Anyway, most of the words struggle to get from my brain to the paper. Writing is a marriage of the mind and fingertips on the keyboard, and like a marriage, it can be a challenge.

The Nightmare

I was reading and dozing on the sofa at our daughter's home. They were expected back from a college parents' weekend that evening. I brought their high school daughter (who stayed with us, along with their dog Charley) back to their own house so she could get her things ready for school the next day.

The plane was delayed, and when her parents rolled in at 2 a.m., waking me up from a deep sleep, I told them I was staying on the sofa. I'd go home in the morning.

I woke up around 4 a.m. to use the bathroom and then went back to dreamland, literally. I usually have bizarre dreams when I fall back to sleep in the early morning hours. And I did that morning. I was in the driver's seat of a car (not mine), talking with a strange man who was sitting in the back seat. I don't know what we talked about or where this was, but all of a sudden I told him I needed to leave. And he said, "No." So I reached over to the door handle, as I felt an arm grab me around the shoulders from behind.

In a panic, I knew he would overpower me and I needed to scream, so at the top of my lungs, I yelled, "Help!" I woke myself up, realizing I really did yell "Help!"—so loud that my daughter and son-in-law woke up in a cold sweat. I heard Sharon's voice at the top of the stairs, asking, "Mom, are you ok?"

"I'm so sorry, Sharon. It was just a nightmare."

The next day, she told me I traumatized her. "Imagine how I felt, hearing a blood curdling scream from my seventy-four-year-old mother. I was afraid there was something medically wrong, and I wouldn't know what to do; or that you fell off the sofa."

Fell off the sofa? Their sofa is so soft and low to the ground, I need all my strength to pull myself into a standing position, grabbing the glass topped coffee table—praying I won't smash my forehead into the glass. So, falling off the sofa was an impossibility. Careening into the glass was very possible.

Fruit Flies

Everyone knows what a fruit fly is—those pesky microscopic bugs which like to swarm around over-ripe bananas. Well, recently we were invaded with them. I blame it on the fruit smoothies I decided to add to our diet. Neither of us are big fruit eaters, but I found the fruit went down a lot faster if I blended the blueberries and added a banana. So, I wasn't quick to throw out the over-ripe bananas, not realizing I was providing a breeding ground for these annoying fruit flies.

I consulted Google, shocked to see a million solutions to get rid of them, naturally. I put bowls of apple cider vinegar with a few drops of dish detergent in strategic places. "What the hell is that awful smell?" asked Paul when he came home from the gym.

"I am trapping fruit flies—you know, those tiny gnats you seem to think are overtaking our house." I showed him the traps. "I already killed two."

The fruit flies, miniscule as they are, must have a brain. They seemed to catch on to my plan to exterminate them, as I found a few walking along the edge of the rim on the bowl, careful not to venture in. I was going to flick them in with my finger, but that would be cheating. I upped my game, and added a piece of a rotting banana to each bowl.

"I think I'd rather have the fruit-flies," said Paul. "Every room in the house smells and has this disgusting bowl of yellow liquid with something gross floating around in it."

I went to plan B the next day, dumping the bowls' contents into the sink. I saw another cool idea online. Into a skinny Budweiser beer glass, I poured about two inches of apple cider vinegar with a couple drops of dish detergent. I rolled up a sheet of typing paper into a funnel, and inserted it into the glass. A couple days later, I counted seven flies floating in the vinegar.

I told my sister, who replied, "Are you kidding me?—you didn't know that about vinegar traps?"

"Can you just let me have my moment?"

Our granddaughter visited a couple days later, and I couldn't wait to show her a potential science project. "Grandma, you can order all kinds of little zapper gadgets on Amazon—fruit flies gone for good!"

My ego zapped twice in one week.

Pebbles

There's a lot of frightening stuff going on in the world. I find it ironic that we watch the suffering (in great detail) on TV in real time—horrified. And yet, when the news is over, we quickly flip the channel on the remote to a sports event or a movie, without blinking an eye.

We have learned to compartmentalize quite well. I guess it is a good thing, for our own mental health. Otherwise, how could we function? But it bothers me. I don't like feeling helpless when I look into the faces of the victims, especially the children.

Am I naive to have hope that the world can change? For my part, I can pray that we all seek the truth, vote for honest leaders, and not lose our voices. But is there nothing else?

I like to imagine we are all like pebbles, making ripples when dropped into a pond. If everyone made positive ripples, I know the world order would change, eventually. I don't want to be the pebble that sits for centuries on a sandy beach, having no effect on my fellow human beings.

I hope that kindness becomes as contagious as the flu.

Partners in Keeping Me Sane

These partners are humor and prayer. Getting older has taught me that even the most awful things in life often have a thread of humor, tiny as it may seem.

Some may view laughter in bad situations as odd, dismissive, or even callous. I find it a coping mechanism and a healing balm, all in one.

I think that prayer probably has different meanings to different people. For me, it's a conversation with God. I've had people say to me, "You're a worrier, aren't you?" And yes, I guess I am. I just turned seventy-five, and I'm still working on trust, but at least I know where to go for my peace and reassurance.

Occasionally when I pray, I listen to the "Ave Maria" by Josh Groban or "The Prayer," by Celine Dion and Andrea Bocelli through my ear buds. With the volume turned up, the experience is heavenly—hopefully worth the destruction of my ear drums.

Time to Say Adieu

I think it's time I ended this book. I'm sure you're in the mood for some historical fiction by this time, or maybe a mystery. I hope that reading my book made the weight of your problems a little lighter.

Laugh at the mundane, cry at the tragic.
Be patient.
Keep smiling until the laughter finds its way back.
It will.

ACKNOWLEDGMENTS

I want to thank Cindy Hall for reading my latest work with a critical eye and helping me organize my thoughts into a coherent book.

Determining whether an essay tickled the funny bone of someone in my target audience was accomplished by watching the reactions of those who read my first drafts. Humor is so subjective, but I knew when something fell flat.

My long suffering husband read countless pages, and aside from warning me that he might need to retain a lawyer, he good-naturedly went along with the anecdotes which included him.

Now that we live in Rhode Island, I am grateful for my long distance relationship with The Rehoboth Beach Writers Guild and Maribeth Fischer, its Executive Director. Their encouragement has been invaluable in my writing life. Our weekly writer chats on Zoom, hosted by Cindy Hall, are a writer's dream. We talk about our writing journeys and the marketing of the fruits of our work, in the comfort of our homes. Thank you also to Crystal Heidel for hosting another weekly Zoom, where we write with the sound muted for forty-five minutes, getting positive vibes from our fellow writers.

Thank you to the Association of Rhode Island Authors for informing us of services offered, and making us aware of venues to showcase our work.

I can't leave out my dear friends and family. Without you, I would not have the material to craft a story; and more importantly, the love and encouragement to keep writing.